MACHU MY PICCHU

ALSO BY IRIS BAHR

Dork Whore: My Travels through Asia as a Twenty-Year-Old Pseudo-Virgin

Machu My Picchu

Searching for **Sex**, **Sanity**, and a **Soul Mate**
in South America

Iris Bahr

skirt!®

Guilford, Connecticut
An imprint of Globe Pequot Press

To my close friends and immediate family, who will most likely stop speaking to me after reading this book. I thank you for the emotional scars you have caused because my artistic endeavors would not be possible without them. All my love and gratitude. Seriously.

skirt!® is an attitude . . . spirited, independent, outspoken, serious, playful and irreverent, sometimes controversial, always passionate.

Copyright © 2011 by Iris Bahr

skirt!® is a registered trademark of Morris Publishing Group, LLC, and is used with express permission.

Text design: Sheryl Kober

Layout: Kirsten Livingston

Maps by Piper Verlag

Turbulation image on page 85 by Samuels Advertising

Certain events, names, locations, defining details, and body types have been changed to protect the guilty.

Library of Congress Cataloging-in-Publication Data is available on file.

ISBN 978-0-7627-7277-3

Printed in the United States of America

10 9 8 7 6 5 4 3 2 1

Contents

Prologue

O CAPTAIN, MY CAPTAIN

Dear Brown University Board of Admissions,

First I'd like to commend you on receiving five stars in both the social and academic categories in the prestigious BIG FAT BLUE GUIDE TO AMERICAN COLLEGES. I'm sure the ranking is well deserved. I have always loved school and, as my grades can attest, have excelled in my studies. Your academic offerings are the main reason I am applying to your wondrous institution. That and the fact that I have been somewhat miserable and lost in my life to date, thanks to my parents' scarring and messy divorce, two years of mind-numbing service in the Israel Defense Forces, and a fear of men that has led to my inability to have sexual intercourse with the opposite sex. (I don't mean to imply that I have had successful intercourse with the same sex. Not my bag. Not that I'm judging. The Big

Fat Blue Guide mentioned you have several lesbian clubs and organizations, and I commend you on that as well.)

I am happy to report, however, that, thanks to both a highly adventurous six-month solo backpacking journey through Asia and a large garden vegetable, I've managed to overcome my fear of intercourse and have been having industrial amounts of sex with various cooperative parties in the greater Tel Aviv area. Consequently, I feel like I am ready to embark on the next stage of my growth as a dysfunctional, off-kilter woman, and I wholeheartedly believe that Brown University is the best place for this growth—mentally, psychologically, and, most importantly, intellectually.

Thank you ahead of time for your acceptance. ~~Trust me, you don't want to say no. An opportunity like me does not come along every day.~~

Sincerely,
Iris (eereese) Bahr

My yes letter arrives several months later. I can't tell if Ima[1] is happy or devastated—she basically says she's happy while simultaneously sobbing and moaning. I can't blame her. She spent six months waiting for me to get back from my little jaunt to Asia, and now, after only a few months back at home, I tell her I'm leaving again. Leaving her. Leaving everything actually. For a substantial chunk of time.

---

1 Ima: Mother. Aba: Father. Hypersexed Neurotic: Me.

Yes, unlike my Israeli comrades, who are about to start their mind-numbing academic experience at good ole Tel Aviv University, replete with ugly '50s architecture, jaded bitter students, and incessant teacher strikes, I'm off to begin my lustrous, Ivy League education in picturesque New England, where gorgeous, sweatered intellectual men will pleasure me while spouting Heidegger witticisms. Where the handsomest, smartest boy of the bunch, who's also blessed with an athletic physique, will fall in love with me and take me on midnight walks through campus, a copy of *Paradise Lost* in his hand, and we will kiss as I caress his cashmere sweater, and he will tell me I am "exotic" and "worldly" and "much more interesting than those boring American girls," and he will marvel at my sexual prowess without knowing the laborious history behind it, and we will spend hours gazing lovingly into each other's eyes, thrilled to be in each other's brilliant presence, and he will propose marriage, and I will bring him back to Tel Aviv, and my friends will marvel at his amazing head of hair[2] and his fantastic teeth and no-smoking policy, and we will get married on the beach and have lots of well-read, instantly intellectual babies, and I will be content and unafraid till the end of my days.

Ima can't blame me. After all, this whole Ivy League college thing was my dad's idea. In his mind, his daughter owed it to him and the world at large to do what he "never had the chance to do." (He spent his college years juggling sixteen jobs and building Zion from scratch.) And so he urged me to take

---

2   Most Israeli men lose their hair by age 25, hence the country is filled with shaved heads and hairy backs.

time out of my disappointingly non-hectic military schedule on base to apply to colleges in America. So I did.

Why wouldn't I? College in America sounded divine. Especially to a miserable, pseudo-virgin[3] army sergeant in the midst of an alienation crisis of epic proportions, who spent every waking minute trying to get laid but found it emotionally and physically impossible to do so. How could I *not* want to escape my current reality rut and drown myself in large pools of DIFFERENT?

I already had pool A ready to go: my trip to Asia, where I planned on decongesting my bio tunnel in exotic locales. I would then dive into pool B: American college, where I would enjoy the fruits of my Asian labors and indulge in the aforementioned Heidegger witticism-copulation combo.

I had no idea how to get into pool B, and so, after an especially sexually frustrating/alienating night shift that involved ten hours of boring intelligence feeds and a news alert that Iran was being naughty again, I raced over to the English bookstore in downtown Tel Aviv, located at the end of a urine-drenched alleyway,[4] and bought the *Big Fat Blue Guide to American Colleges.*

---

3   My virginity was only briefly alleviated by a Moroccan paratrooper named Patrick, whose penis was of soup-can proportions and whose presence inside me I could only tolerate for several seconds.

4   I am proud to say that the quality of urine stench in selected alleys in Tel Aviv is unparalleled. Unlike New York City, where the pee smell is confounded by garbage, car exhaust, rat excrement, and millions of humans, Tel Aviv is relatively unpopulated. Hence the urine is not contaminated by other factors. Couple that with the highly humid climate, scorching Middle Eastern sun, and sidewalks that have never felt the loving touch of a garden hose, and the result is a sharp acidic pee odor of the purest kind. I hope the city is one day recognized for this accomplishment.

I learned from said guide that some schools were "party schools," some were "safety schools," some were uptight, others were Jesuit, some had frats, others had crew teams. (I didn't know what a crew team was, but it sounded wonderfully proletarian.) But out of all these schools, only one had both five stars for academics and five stars for social life. It was called Brown University, situated in picturesque Providence, Rhode Island. Unlike its uptight Ivy sisters, the BFBG explained, Brown preferred "off-kilter" applicants over straitlaced students and WASPy boarding-school kids. It was considered the most edgy and experimental of the Ivies and the most risqué, a virtual collegiate heaven on earth with a gorgeous campus and stunning architecture. It even had a building just like the one Robert Sean Leonard jumped out of right after the *Midsummer Night's Dream* fiasco.

I scrolled down to the application requirements. Shit. Preferred applicants had to have perfect grades *and* have engaged in at least three unique extracurricular activities during their high school years. What the hell were extracurricular activities? Herzelia High didn't have any "extracurricular activities." The entire school consisted of nine asbestos shacks and a bomb shelter that doubled as a gymnasium. The sample activities the guide listed were all very American—like cheerleading (a concept foreign to the people of Israel), and debate teams (a concept familiar to the people of Israel, only they don't really do it in sporty teams; it's more an existential necessity that involves "debaters" shouting their arguments in unison). Since sex was still too terrifying for me during those years, the only activity I did after school was go to a small punk rock club called The Penguin with my best friend, Ronit. She and I were the only two punk rockers who kept their natural hair color, didn't smoke or do drugs, and had their mothers drop them off at the entrance.

How on earth was I going to compete with glee-filled debating cheerleaders? But wait. What about the army? That's extracurricular, right? I could put "sergeant in Israeli army" on the application—but then they're going to think that I'm some über-militant extremist who has wet dreams about renting a couple of shuttle buses and transferring the entire Palestinian population to Fez or Detroit. Not that I don't have those dreams sometimes.

Kidding.

Kind of.

No really, I'm kidding. No such dreams. I'm for co-existence. Two state solution, all that good stuff. Let's not go there right now, though, because this is about me. *My* needs. *My* existence. And the beginning of *my* amazing new life! (Not that I don't care about anybody else's life, but you get the point.)

Why does the prospect of leaving home again excite and calm me so? Most people would be sad to leave their family, their friends, their home. But those people are well adjusted. And loved. And loving. Jesus, this line of thinking is bringing me down. The point is, home makes me anxious, and when the familiar is icky, the unfamiliar is always an improvement.

PROVIDENCE

1

CARTON OF KENTS

Aba had suggested that Ima and I fly to New York so we could drive up to Providence together. The prospect of sitting in a car with both my parents is harrowing. I have many a tense childhood memory of sitting in the back of my dad's massive black Crown Vic,[5] an odd cherry smell emanating from the hole-ridden gray upholstered seats, while my parents fought like two crazies in the front, chain-smoking Kents in perfect unison. That's literally all I remember. Fighting and smoking. Sometimes just smoking. But never fighting without smoking.

Our weekend drives to see my brother at his institution upstate were the worst.[6] Not only was I nervous about the

---

5 The largest sedan on the market. For my European readers not familiar with American cars (since you are too busy cramming into your little Peugeots and Fiats and whatever other little toy cars they've invented that you can park in your kitchen) the Crown Victoria is a masterwork of American grandiosity and a staple car for every police officer in the greater New York area.

6 My brother has autism confounded by a severe mental retardation that really can't be defined or categorized. He says few words, and, while he can recognize us and says our names when prompted, he requires full care and is enveloped in a world that we tragically cannot enter.

fighting, I was nervous about seeing my brother. His home was a brick cottage situated among dozens of similar cottages on the institution grounds. It had yellow linoleum floors and plastic furniture and smelled like orange juice, antiseptic, and tragedy. The other kids in his cottage frightened me—some hit themselves really hard, others stared at me oddly, others screamed and groaned. My brother did all of the above, which made me cry the hardest. Funny, you'd think I'd cry less as I got older, but I only cried more, perhaps out of an increasing awareness of how heartbreaking and irreversible his condition was.

After particularly tough visits, in which my brother would scream-repeat a mantra that neither Ima nor Aba could silence, we would kiss my brother goodbye and re-enter the Crown Vic, whereupon my parents would take all their sadness and anger and frustration and helplessness and guilt out on each other for the entire drive home while I stuck my heavy head out the window and sucked the air blasting past as if it could leaf-blow my pain away.

Isn't it time to erase that ancient memory? I mean, what the hell am I worried about? My parents are on great terms these days—so great it actually annoys the shit out of me. Why is it that parents always treat each other like fecal matter during their child's crucial developmental years, but the minute their child is old enough to not be as susceptible to damage by ugly parental dynamics, the parents suddenly forgive and forget and become buddies, leaving the now already-fucked-up child to try and heal the wounds inflicted by the parents during the formative years while the happy parents hang out with each other's new spouses and wonder what the hell is wrong with their dysfunctional grown-up offspring?

But that's irrelevant. What *is* relevant is that I'm not a little kid in the backseat anymore. I'm a BIG kid in the backseat. Which would be manageable except that Aba still has the same Crown Vic, which may not work in my Pavlovian favor.

❧

Ima and I board the plane and head down the offensively narrow aisle toward our seat. The last time we flew together was when we left America to come to Israel. Things have changed. For one, I don't have to sit in the smoking section. And I don't look like a boy this time around.

Let me explain.

It was many summers ago. I was thirteen.

In honor of our leaving the United Suck of America and moving to the Holy Land, my mom decided that I would get a haircut. Which I didn't mind. I rarely got haircuts as a child. Maybe because once my hair reaches shoulder length it seems to say, "Fuck it, I'm stopping right here." Not that I wanted longer hair back then. I mean, Judith Eisenberg had hair down to her knees, and she just looked like a horse with decent features. In essence, my hair had been the same length since I was six years old, and so I felt no qualms about jumping on the new-beginning bandwagon, telling Carlo the tight-panted haircutter (who, despite having male genitalia, managed to sport a remarkably well-etched camel toe) to chop it all off. And so he did.

I felt great about my new cut. It was as if all the toxic memories that had seeped into my follicles had been expelled from my system, and I was ready to start my fresh and sassy pixie-like existence in the Middle East.

And so Ima, my Siamese cat, Porsche, and I hopped into a cab and headed to the airport. Porsche was as excited to get out of the Bronx as I was—even more so, considering that for the last few years he was unable to enjoy even the minimal perks of being a cat, like sleeping, shitting in peace, and not thinking. Not only did he have to deal with unfun surroundings that involved lots of sobbing, yelling, dramatic hand gestures, and general chaos, he also had to function as my confidante, my weeping pillow, and my best friend. We were one step away from finding him face down in the kitty litter with a suicide note attached to his catnip-soiled whiskers.

Porsche had a pointy face, a lean physique, and a disturbingly human way of communicating. His meows were long, powerful yet nebbishy, as if he were channeling Woody Allen after a bar fight. And while he was thrilled we were leaving for better pastures, Porsche was not happy about being in a tiny cage, and he groaned all the way to the airport and continued to groan as my mom and I approached the check-in counter.

The thin-lipped check-in woman asked if he was sedated. I said no. She glared at me as if I were an adult. An idiotic adult. My mother stood behind me, frantically gesticulating and smoking. I tried to calm her down, but I was freaking out, and my abilities were limited. The airline monsters were threatening to throw Porsche in cargo; they had no sedatives, and Porsche was now groaning in twenty-second-long spurts. The only option, we were told, was to buy an extra seat. My mom rushed to the counter and paid the fee, God bless her.

By the time we boarded the plane, it was already full. My mother and I hauled our sweaty bodies toward our seats, Porsche's groans reverberating through the aisles. I prayed that he would relax once we got situated, and I could proceed to my usual in-flight activity: holding a vomit bag to my mouth and wondering why other people were not vomiting along with me.

I placed Porsche near the window and poked my hand through the tiny cage door to pet him. He let out a massive "Don't touch me I'm not in the mood you skanky whore" moan that sent my hand right back out. I covered the cage with my sweatshirt, hoping the darkness would calm him, but to no avail.

The plane started down the runway. I looked over at my mother. She was white as a sheet and so emotionally exhausted from the whole ordeal (not just the last three hours but the last three years) that I feared she would ooze off the seat like an overcooked vermicello. I wanted this dreaded flight to be over, and we still had eleven hours left.

The feline groaning didn't cease. In fact, it got so bad at one point that Porsche started to lose his voice. The woman behind us asked if our baby was sick. (Yes, she thought we had a baby there. What kind of baby is beyond me.)

Somewhere over the Atlantic I turned to see that Ima had somehow managed to fall asleep. As luck would have it, her anxiety had reached such an exhausting point that her body just shut down. I, however, opted to stay in the perpetual awake-anxiety stage. But I couldn't take the moaning anymore.

I decided to take Porsche out of the cage and into the bathroom for a respite. He could walk around, stretch his legs, perhaps watch the blue fluid circle down the metal toilet. I scooped up his alarmingly warm body and nestled him close to my chest. He was panting like a dog and had an "I fucking hate flying!" glaze in his eye. I rushed to the bathroom and was just about to open the door when a loud voice boomed behind me.

"BOY!"

Probably some Hasidic Jew leaning over some self-hating Israeli with his legs in the aisle.

"BOY! STOP!"

I opened the door to the bathroom. Porsche's salvation was near.

"BOY! STOP RIGHT NOW! DO NOT ENTER THE BATHROOM!"

I turned around. The head flight attendant, a lanky yet stern ex-commando type, was staring at me as if I were cradling a dirty bomb.

It finally hit me. I had short hair. Really short hair. From the back, I looked like a boy. A bad, dirty bomb–carrying boy. I smiled sheepishly and waited for him to correct his gender assessment once he saw my face. He did not.

"BOY, GET BACK IN YOUR SEAT, AND PUT THE CAT BACK IN THE CAGE!"

Porsche groaned in agony. I took my Jamie Lee Curtis–self back to my seat and put Porsche back into his cage. I wanted nothing more than to crawl in there with him.

I spent the rest of the flight whispering sweet nothings in Porsche's ear, eating paprika-enhanced pretzels (exclusive to El Al Israel airlines), and fielding questions from the woman behind me on the pains of childbirth. By the time we landed in Israel, Porsche wasn't the only one panting and drooling. My mother, on the other hand, was remarkably well rested and relaxed. Okay, maybe just well rested. One can still dream, though.

❧

Here I am now on a flight once again, albeit a much quieter one. No Porsche to roar my head off, fewer Orthodox Jews than God would have liked, and a wonderful little pill in my hand called Travamin.[7]

As I hinted earlier, flying has been my bodily nightmare since the time I could spew out my own juices; every bump of turbulence sending my gut into a flurry of gastric doom and my mouth into the air sickness bag as if water from the fountain of youth was locked inside its paper fibers.

But one day, out of the blue, as if modern medicine had just been invented moments earlier, my mom said to

---

7   Don't get me wrong; I'm not a pill popper. On the contrary, I am anti-pill. I believe in suffering through natural pain and letting the body take care of itself, even though this way of living has proven completely ineffective to date, as my premature gray hairs and frequent health issues can attest. And let's not forget what happened to Bob Marley.

me, "Why don't you take some Travamin?"—as if she knew about this salvatory remedy for years and simply hadn't thought about it as she watched her daughter spew up her spleen every time she boarded an aircraft.

Travamin proved to be a miracle drug and the first step toward making flying bearable. (I later discovered another technique that actually made it pleasurable, but more about that later.) Gone were my days of suffering the entire flight in upchuckity. I now spent my sky-time chatting and entertaining the passengers, flirting with the gay flight attendants in exchange for inter-meal snacks, and changing socks or entire outfits to give the other members of the flight a more festive viewing experience.

ლ

JFK hasn't changed since we last saw it, which for some reason puts me and Ima in good spirits. The sad fact that I am relocating for the foreseeable future has obviously not sunk in yet, and so we giddily head toward immigration.

"They're going to pull me aside, I know they will," my mom declares with doom.

"Why would they pull you aside?" I ask, as I always do, fully aware that my mom has this theory that she is always singled out by law enforcement and is verbally assaulted by various immigration officers.

"They're going to put me in a room, yell at me, and take away my green card."

This is a good time to inform you that my mother has a flair for the dramatic. Every altercation my mother recounts always has several key elements that ring of early *Law and Order* episodes: The officer is always intimidating, always aggressive for no particular reason, and always uses the word "lady" an exorbitant number of times in a very hostile, Brooklyn-accented manner.

In reality they never take my mother's green card away, and I have no idea if they yell at her and call her "lady" nine times, but she does always spend at least two hours at immigration, and I can't for the life of me figure out why. Why would they target a five-foot-tall Bulgarian woman with gentle blue eyes and no history of illegal activity?

"I'm telling you, they're gonna haul me in that little room and yell and scream at me and search me and then take my green card away, and then I will have problems visiting you and Ami." She begins to spiral into a state of heightened anxiety.

"Ima, they are not going to take away your green card. They never take away your green card. They have bigger problems to worry about like arms smuggling and illegal citrus."

I can see the panic in her eyes and realize to what extent her anxiety is self-induced.

"Stop making yourself nervous all the time!" I snap.

Of course my snapping makes her even more nervous, and so she enters phase two: the guilt-inducing segment of the anxiety attack.

"Don't snap at your mother. It's hard enough for me to have you leave me like this, and now I have to deal with the immigration Gestapo."

Her technique works, and I instantly feel horrible. I mean, of course my mom is nervous and is projecting her fears upon well-trained government employees. I should be more understanding.

I give her a hug. "Nobody is going to take away your green card, okay? Please stop making up these horrible scenarios. They're not helpful, and I'm as anxious as you are."

She nods, teary eyed, and we hug for a sweet moment. I guide her toward the GREENCARD HOLDERS line then skip to my US CITIZENS line, full of plump and happy Americanos proud of their citizenship.

The immigration official is of possible Samoan descent. I smile. He furrows his doughy cheeks.

"You haven't been here in a while," he says, as if he missed me.

"I've been living in Israel." I reassure him, "It's nothing personal."

He laughs. "What brings you back?" he says. One of his teeth is gray. Unfortunate.

"I'm starting college."

"Where?"

"Brown University."

"Oooh, fancy, one of those Ivy League schools. Good for you." He stamps my passport.

I take it back, grinning like a child who just received a "YOU'RE A STAR!" sticker from her teacher. The kind with raspberry smell.

I head to baggage claim to wait for our suitcases. They all look the same. Why can't the luggage companies expand the fucking color spectrum? Is it really only red and black? The only people that have it right are the Hasidic Jews— they have extra large suitcases made especially for them. I guess nine children need a bunch of clothes, and better to concentrate them in one massive four-by-four suitcase than nine small ones.

The man next to me picks up every single black suitcase that passes and looks at the tag like an idiot. I shake my head.

"Same problem?" he asks, wanting to commiserate with another black-suitcase owner.

"I have a black suitcase, but I don't have to worry."

"How's that?" he asks, incredulous.

"My mother has a system."

"A system?"

"A system of markings."

He looks at me confused. What are these markings I speak of?

The first of our suitcases emerges from the abyss. It is indeed a black suitcase like all the others, but there are 26 pink ribbons tied around the handle. One pink ribbon would be cheesy, but 26 pink ribbons is foolproof—even for really dumb blind people.

"Ahh!" he says. "I know what to do next time!"

"Don't use pink," I say in a surprisingly stern voice. "Then everyone is going to use pink ribbons, and we'll all be screwed."

"Of course, of course!" he says, pink with fear. "I wouldn't want to screw up the system."

"Thank you," I say as he picks up another black suitcase for naught.

I wait for my mother for another hour. Still no sign. My dad is probably freaking out. I know he's already waiting for us outside—he's chronically early just like my mom (and me). He also cannot comprehend the word "delay," which means he probably thinks we're both dead.

Another hour and a half, still no sign of her. By now I've ripped off all the pink ribbons in an anxious frenzy. Like mother, like daughter. Like father.

Finally she arrives.

"What happened? What took you so long?" I ask, pale with worry.

"They took my green card."

"What? No, they didn't."

My mom looks thrilled. They really did.

"Why are you so happy?"

"I knew it! I knew they would take it! I was right!"

My mother couldn't be happier that ten years of anxiety over some possible event were now justified.

"So what does that mean? You can't come visit me?"

"No, I just have to get a visa. It's not a problem." She glances at the shredded pink ribbons on the ground and puts her arm around me. It's getting late, and we have a long drive ahead of us. "Your dad is probably worried sick. He's always worried about everything, poor man."

I can't help but laugh. She looks at me and realizes how absurd her last statement was. I grab our suitcases and we head toward the exit for the next phase of the journey.

2

THE FALL

The drive isn't nearly as traumatizing as I thought it'd be. For one, Ima asks me to sit up front. What's more, Aba asks me to drive! No more backseat horrors, my friends—I am driving the Crown Vic. I am in control of the boat! I may not fully reach the gas pedal and can barely see over the dashboard, but I have my hands on the wheel and it is grand.

We roar up I-95 toward Providence, the colorful leaves of autumn whooshing past—reds, yellows, browns. I haven't experienced autumn in years. Israel has two seasons: hot and kind of rainy for a week. Come to think of it, I had actually forgotten autumn even existed. My mind had somehow obliterated any pleasant seasons from my memory bank, leaving me with the impression that my entire caca childhood had transpired in winter months only. (The fact is, crappy childhood memories pack more punch when they take place against a backdrop of corpse-like trees swaying in icy winds rather than a bikini fruit-punch pool party.)

We spend twenty minutes oohing and ahhing at the foliage, and then everyone goes quiet. At first, the silence of the drive is soothing, but, as is always the case with neurotic individuals, too much quiet lets the brain go to those fun scary places, and I watch in the rear view mirror as my mother's face transforms from nature-based awe to separation melancholy. She's doing her best to conceal her pain. I turn on the radio, quickly moving the dial from suicidal Wagner on the staticky classical station to cheesy pop on Z100. "Easy Lover" is playing, and I sing along with forceful zest and vigor, but Ima is too sad for even Phil and that black guy from Earth, Wind, and Fire to pep her up.

೮ɔ

Three hours and one speeding ticket later (Aba's attempts at "We're Israeli, what do we know?" didn't quite work on the Connecticut state trooper), we roll onto the Brown campus. It's a stunning expanse of majestic buildings, cute cottages, and a shwarma joint. The map shows that my dormitory, Pembroke, is nestled at the end of a picturesque footpath off Waterman Street. After some frustrating circling around the campus, we finally find it. Dad pulls over angrily, pressing the hazard lights button with force.

He starts unloading my suitcases, and I promptly start to bawl. Reality hits me the way I wish it had three days earlier, when it would have coincided with the peak of my mother's breakdown. This time I'm really saying goodbye. Not for a six month sex-romp through Asia but for four years. In Providence. Where I have no friends. Who has the energy to make new friends? I'm too old for this shit. What the fuck was I *thinking*? What's wrong with ugly '50s Tel Aviv architecture and jaded students, for Chrissake?!

"Are you all right?" my father asks, choking up.

"I'm just sad to say goodbye," I say, tears in full flow now.

My dad wraps my mother and me in a strong embrace. Now we're all sobbing. You'd think I was being shipped to Nam.

He pulls out a mini pack of Kleenex from his pocket. I stop crying as shock sets in. My dad *never* uses Kleenex. He was always one of those men who had the unfortunate affinity for handkerchiefs, into which he would blow his nose and then neatly fold into a lovely square and stuff back into his pocket. For years, my mother and I made fun of this habit. He always got offended by our mockery, earnestly launching into a shpiel about how he was only following family tradition; his father and his father's father, all the way back to the Inquisition in Spain, all used handkerchiefs. I countered with a shpiel about the bubonic plague and hand-washing and how certain things were best left to extinctify themselves. For years, I tried to lure him over to the world of tissues and other disposable items but to no avail. And now here he is, pulling a travel pack of Kleenex out of his pocket. I laugh. My parents look at me, first confused, then relieved I'm not sobbing anymore. A sudden urge to head upstairs into my new world washes over me. I reassure them both that I don't need help with my suitcases (lie), I'd rather we keep the goodbyes short (truth), and I'll be fine (who the fuck knows, let's be optimistic).

And so they board the boat, light up their Kents, and drive off, leaving a plume of cherry-tinted smoke in their wake.

3

GOUDA TO GO

Unlike the picturesque stone cottages in the "Come to Brown!" pamphlet, Pembroke is a gray brick cube that smells like a 7-Eleven.[8] I lug my bags up to the second floor and down the hallway toward room 207. I can't help but notice several crusty stains on the carpeting. You'd think for $50,000 per student a year, they could afford to replenish the carpeting on a yearly/monthly basis. And where the hell is everybody? Apparently the clan of cardiganned hotties is out pleasuring Robin Williams at some undisclosed location. That's the curse of being chronically early. You are always prepared for something that hasn't happened yet. And by the time it does happen, you are so frustrated for

---

8   As those who have been in a 7-Eleven know, the smell is a nauseating combination of beef jerky, vanilla flavoring, and white-trash desperation. I hate the smell of vanilla. I get that from my mom. She hates it as much as she hates Nicolas Cage. But not as much as she hates Tom Hanks. Or Robin Williams. She *really* hates Robin Williams.

having waited so long that the latecomers are all fresher and better prepared than you are.

The door to room 207 is slightly ajar. I push it open. Nobody home. I guess my roommate hasn't arrived yet. My sneakers make a suction-sticky sound. The carpet has been replaced by shiny, violet-black linoleum. Is proper flooring not allocated in the college décor budget either? How about some nice hardwood to make the kids feel like they're getting their money's worth? Jesus.

Inside are two super-narrow twin beds on opposite ends of the room, glued to equally tiny wood desks. I dump my things onto the mini-bed and cautiously arrange my underwear in the sketchy pine drawer. Note to self: must buy drawer lining. Who knows what lurked in here beforehand. Probably the same creatures that caused the carpet stains.

"Welcome to Pembroke!" a voice squeaks. A small boy is leaning against my door frame.

"Oh, thanks!"

The boy has a sweet acne-ridden face. Must be accompanying an older sibling.

"I'm Jeremy. Room 204."

What? This kid couldn't be over 13. His voice hasn't even changed yet.

"Oh. Wow. Nice to meet you."

"You must be the international student from Israel, right? I went to Israel for my bar mitzvah. It was awesome!"

Jeremy is joined by a tall lanky redhead with no eyelashes.

"This is my roommate, Gus. He's from New Canaan."

I have a feeling New Canaan bears no resemblance to the original Canaan, whence I hail.

"Hi, Gus."

"We heard your roommate is from Holland!" Gus cries in prepubescent glee.

The boys high-five. Ahh . . . Dutch chicks.

"So you were in the army, right?" Jeremy asks knowingly.

God, this conversation sounds familiar. "Yes."

I wait for the "Ooh, you must be tough. Can you kill us with your bare hands? You must know krav maga . . . " etc., etc.

"Holy shit, you must be old enough to buy us beer!" Jeremy squeals.

Gus cheers as if the messiah had arrived carrying orgasms in his shirt pocket.

"You want me to buy you beer?" I ask, confused. "Why?"

"Cuz *you're* old enough to buy us alcohol! We're still under-aged!"

"Yeah, you're old!"

Ah. I had forgotten about the whole "drinking age" in America. There is no such thing in Israel. We are drafted into the military the minute we turn 18 and are handed automatic weaponry. I guess deeming us too young to drink would be a little ridiculous. Either way, the boys look at me with a newfound respect, and I want to fit in, so I smile. "Sure, no problem."

The tots do a victory dance. I politely shut the door as their conversation turns to darts and Jenna Jameson.

☙

Upon ensuring that all my underwear are properly aligned and able to welcome the various bacteria into their cotton folds, I put on my flip-flops and head down the hallway to the showers, which consist of lemon yellow tile (re-grouting budget, anyone?) and extremely strong jets of water. I release a hefty sigh as the smoke and anxiety wash off my body, then head back to the room to wait for roomster.

From down the hallway, I see the door is now closed. Carrie has arrived! As I get closer, I notice a strong scent of men's deodorant wafting out from within. She's getting it on already, good for her! Nice to know we're both sexual beings eager to satisfy our college fantasies. How fun! Maybe we can make one of those little signs cool girls in dorms have that alert the other "stay out, sex happening inside!" Maybe she could write one in Dutch too, just for shits and giggles!

I don't want to disturb the copulatory fiesta, but I am standing in nothing but a towel and fear the tots will come out and want to see my boobies. I knock gently.

"Come in!" says a raspy woman's voice with an absurdly slight Dutch accent—(the Dutch may not have spice or flavor or distinctive facial features, but they do have tulips and weed and a ridiculously amazing command of the English language).

I open the door to find a doughy hand applying deodorant to a very large armpit. It's Carrie—and Carrie's armpit. Her body is huge. Her head is equally huge. She's built like a house. A truck. A trailer. Whatever vehicle or massive object large humans can resemble. I have never seen a woman on steroids, but Carrie is definitely steroidal. Or just fat. But a different kind of fat. Hard fat. Muscular fat.

"Hi, I'm Carrie," she says.

On Carrie's bed are two large boxes of pizza and what looks like sporting gear, including an orange helmet. She notices my confusion.

"I'm on the field hockey team."

"What is field hockey?" I ask. I am from Israel after all, our sports expertise is limited to machine guns and sailing.

Carrie commences to break down field hockey in the driest fashion possible, including, but not limited to, its rules, regulations, where Brown falls in the Ivy League ranking, how she's from Amsterdam but never smoked pot and never will, and how men's deodorant is more reliable, and would I like to try some?

"I prefer Dove deodorant for *women*," I reply, at which point the conversation screeches to a halt.

Perfect time to get dressed. I toss the towel on the bed, slap on some undies, and begin searching for my feel-good T-shirt. The one I bought in Pushkar, the one that still smells of poverty-ridden sweatshops, cheap dyes, and sweet Indian memories. I suddenly feel Carrie's eyes on my naked back. I turn around. She's staring at me with unveiled lust. It's undeniable. This Mennen-wearing, puck-tossing duchess wants some sweet Jew flesh.

Time to ship out.

4
PLEASE JUST SHUT UP AND GIVE ME MY KEY

Map in hand, I rush over to the housing department, determined to move out of Romper Room into more appropriate housing. The department is a cute little cottage with a cute little mahogany door. Maybe I can move in here. The secretary smiles at me warmly and shows me into the dean's office. His name is Howard Rosen, and he's sitting at his desk touching his Moses-like beard.

Before he can say "My facial hair is inappropriately biblical," I launch into a passionate speech on the inhumanity of housing a grown woman with beer-obsessed toddlers and a large Dutch lesbian.

Howard smiles kindly. "I met Carrie during the international student orientation," he says. "She's a lovely girl."

"She wants to rape me."

"I'm sure it was just a misunderstanding."

"Look, Howard, Dutch intercourse aside, I need to live with people my own age. This is ridiculous."

"But the only people your age are graduate students."

"That sounds great."

"But we'd like you to integrate with students in your class, Iris. Trust me, you'll want to do that."

"But they're 18! They want me to buy them beer!"

"Yes, I imagine they would."

"Please, Dean Howard, find me somewhere else to live. I can't go back to that little bed with that large woman staring at me and the sound of zits popping next door. I won't be able to study, to focus."

"I don't know how I can help you."

"Please, sir *(sniffle)*. I'm going to go crazy in there. I feel like a camp counselor. I was in the Israeli military, for Chrissake—"

Howard's face lights up. "You're the student from Israel?"

"Yes."

"Of course! I'm so sorry I didn't make the connection!! It's so funny, I just got back from Israel two weeks ago. I love Israel!"

The room is suddenly bathed in Howard's Zionist glow. How did I not detect the Holy Land flag waving in his inner wind? God has given me an angle. Thank you, God.

"What a coincidence!" I reply, excited beyond any logical limit. "Where did you visit?"

Howard takes a deep breath, his eyes awash in nostalgia and financial commitment to the state of Israel. "Well,

I spent time on a kibbutz in the '70s, and last year my wife, Cheryl, and I took our kids to Nahariya and also spent some time in Ashdod and Ashkelon visiting Cheryl's relatives. We of course did the Masada expedition and the Dead Sea and also went to the Bahai center in Haifa. It's really amazing. You shouldn't miss it. A lot of locals don't go there; they just take it for granted, but I'm telling you it's absolutely fantastic. Oh and Safed, what a place, what a place! There's this tiny little art gallery off the main strip; they have this wonderful local artist who paints with special paints made from local minerals. She also sculpts. Cheryl bought this lovely salt and pepper shaker set. The only problem is the salt holes are a little big, and we are not a big sodium family. My grandfather was a big salt eater, but we try and keep our spices limited to pepper and paprika. I love paprika on hummus. I've been trying to find a good hummus place here in Providence for the last fifteen years, but it's impossible! If you find one, please let me know. I know you Israelis are resourceful. Cheryl's cousin Dudik from Safed, he's a firecracker of a man. He came here to visit us a few years ago, and I lamented to him, I said, 'Dudik, I miss the hummus you have in Israel,' and he said, 'I will find you a good hummus place, my friend, I promise,' but he ended up having some sort of ankle sprain or tear in his rotator cuff, I don't exactly recall. We had to put him on a flight back to Ben-Gurion a few days earlier than we expected."

After a jewternity he discontinues his monologue and takes a sip of coffee.

What do I do now? Only thing I can do. I put on my best wistful Thank God for the Land of Israel after What

We Went Through in World War II Judaica face, and I wait.

"Come to think of it," he finally says, "I may have room in the Graduate Center. It's a great place to live, and you'll like it much better."

Did he say Grad Center? Students with pubic hair and a drinking license? Yes! Yes!! YES!!

He pulls out a pair of keys from the filing cabinet.

"Thank you, thank you so much!" I say, grabbing them out of his hand.

"Anything to help an Israeli. I should really put you in touch with Cheryl's cousins Malka and Dov in Tkoa—"

I dash out before Malka and Dov's e-mails and fax numbers are shoved in my face and head back to Pembroke to grab my stuff. Thankfully Carrie is in the shower, undoubtedly hand-washing her jockstrap. I pack in ten seconds flat, leave the tots a goodbye note and a six-pack, and head to where I should have been in the first place.

5

WHERE IS JANE FONDA WHEN YOU NEED HER?

Fun factoid: The Graduate Center was designed during the Vietnam War by a famous architect who specialized in what is called anti-riot architecture, which basically means that every aspect of the building is meant to hinder any sort of social interaction that could lead to group gatherings, i.e., sinister anti-war riots or human joy. Consequently, there isn't a single room or hallway that can fit more than two people at a time, the staircases spiral sharply to prevent anyone from accumulating any sort of speed or momentum, and the windows are little crevices that resemble sniper outposts. In other words, it's the perfect place for a new student seeking to socialize and make merry.

But not to panic, I tell myself as I squeeze up the narrow stairs toward my floor. After all, Dean Howard has assigned me to a suite with five other women, none of whom is Dutch or has a penchant for Jewpoon. He assured me of that.

I enter the suite and quickly discover it consists of five cells containing two Asians named Julie and Mindy, a tall blonde named Katharine, a wealthy southern princess named Mia, and a Jamaican sprinter named Carla. They are all 19. So much for graduate students. I should call Malka and Dov and tell them that cousin Howie is a lying rambler.

The girls are welcoming, however, and excited for this surprise addition to their prison. I am equally excited. The Asian chicks are super cute, scurrying around like living breathing Hello Kitty dolls, showing me the bathroom and its amenities in high-pitched enthusiasm. Katherine's expressionless face brings to mind plain yogurt, Mia is part Mexican, part *Gone With the Wind*, and Carla—well, Carla is a warm burst of Jamaican sunshine and the epitome of physical perfection, every muscle toned the way God intended before he invented food and rest.

I learn that these girls were grouped together because they are all pre-med and on a fast track to becoming doctors. They also have a bazillion other interests besides their medical pursuits, including professional instrument playing, karate, and track and field. I suddenly feel like a dumb lump of stale hummus, the kind that has been out for over four seconds and has developed a crust of sorts. (Four seconds is all it takes, try it.)

Jamaican Carla notifies the cell mates that she has an Alpha Phi Alpha step show to attend and invites everyone to join. The other girls look uncomfortable, finding excuses that involve studying, sleep, and tea-time. I have no idea what a step show is, but I find myself gravitating toward Carla, so I say I want to go. She hugs me, thrilled. I can sense she doesn't quite connect with the studious Asians, the oil heiress, or any human with blonde hair. She's just as excited to have found me as I am her.

༄

We walk across campus, which is even more striking at night—the old buildings bathed in dramatic light, Paris style, the smell of pine trees, and the crisp cool air a welcome change from the humid stickiness that plagued my arrival this morning. We approach a stone building. A large group of black students is outside, angry looks on their faces.

"Why are they angry?" I ask Carla.

"That's part of their hazing process for the fraternity. They have to wear hooded black sweatshirts, they aren't allowed to talk to anybody, and they have to carry bricks in their backpacks for weeks. And once that's over they get branded."

"Okay, I didn't understand a word of what you just said."

Carla laughs—a loud, fantasmical, Peter Toshian laugh. "Alpha Phi Alpha is a fraternity. In order to get into the fraternity, you have to go through a bunch of tests that are physically and psychologically exhausting. If you pass, you get into the fraternity, and they take a metal cattle brander—the kind that they brand cows with—and they brand your arm."

Brand your arm? Why would anyone brand their own arm? Do I ask Carla that question? Do I bring up the

Holocaust? No, that would be a downer. And unrelated. Sort of. How about slavery? Didn't slaves get branded? I think so. Why would black people today do it by choice? That's a legitimate question. But who am I to bring up slavery? And why would a bunch of black people want or care to know what a strange Israeli chick thinks about their history and rituals? It's not like they come and lecture me about buying an Audi and listening to Wagner. Best to shut up and view it as a celebratory tattoo and move on.

Carla takes me by the arm and leads me into the large auditorium. "We're late," she says, "but they never start on time, CPT."

"CPT? Is that like GMT?"

"Hah, no, CPT is Colored People's Time," she says, laughing that amazing laugh of hers. "You better learn to deal with it, girl, if you're gonna be hanging out with me!" She laughs some more. I love this woman already.

The auditorium is packed to the gills. I notice I am the only white person there. The thousand black people there also notice.

"Terrell! TERRELL!" Carla yells. From across the way a cute black man in hazing garb smiles and gives her a thumbs up. Guess he just got in. He lifts his shirt sleeve, and lo and behold, bubbling on his flesh, is a huge symbol, still fresh and excruciating.

Ew.

Carla runs over and hugs him. He glances at me from over her shoulder with a "Who's the small white chick?" look on his post-hazed face.

"Terrell, this is my new friend from Israel," Carla says warmly.

Terrell checks me out, a hunger in his eyes that would impress even the most aggressive Israeli sex maniac. He runs back to his posse, winking at me en route.

"Black guys like girls like you," Carla whispers to me, pleased.

"What are girls like me?"

"Girls with a booty."

Finally! Smart men. *And* hung like horses. Fantastic. Who said my *Dead Poets Society* fantasy couldn't have an ethnic version? Bringing Terrell back to Israel would be even cooler! I just have to make sure my friends don't make any awkward *Do you play basketball, brother?* comments when they meet him.

I feel a nudge in my back.

"What are you trying to do, steal our men away from us?"

I turn around to find a very tall black woman with impressive biceps scowling at me.

"Excuse me?" I ask, genuinely perplexed.

"Ignore them," Carla says, staring straight ahead. "They're just jealous."

"You think you can just prance your prissy white ass in here and take our men away?" another tall black woman chimes in.

I turn to Carla for guidance. "It is extremely hard to find a decent black man," she explains. "Most of them are either in jail or on their way to jail, so when a white woman dates a black man they get very resentful."

"I had no idea."

The black woman breathes onto the top of my head. I can't help imagining my pale ass tied to the rafters as black-hooded men with cattle prods brand it with a big W.

Actually, that sounds kind of fun. But I'm no good at ignoring anything or anybody, let alone an angry woman exhaling onto my scalp. I turn around once more.

"I'm sorry, I honestly had no intention of stealing your man. I can't help it if I have a booty."

Carla snorts out a laugh. The girls don't get my attempts at jest. I go the ass-kissing route.

"I imagine they prefer a beautiful tall woman like yourself versus a stubby Israeli like me."

"You're from Israel?" the black woman says in disbelief.

"Yes."

"Oh, that's cool."

I half expect her to mention Dov and Malka, but she turns her attention back to her target demographic, who have now amassed in three perfectly symmetrical lines in the center of the room. Carla smirks, and I vow to avoid all potentially misconstrued eye contact with all black men for the rest of eternity.

Suddenly the lights go out.

Dark silence.

And then the thunderous sound of hundreds of feet pounding in perfect unison. *Boom. Bap. Bap. Boom. Bappity Bap Boom. Bap Bap.*

The lights come up, and the hundred or so hazed induct-ees begin the most amazing "step" routine I have ever seen, a cross between tap dancing, stomping, and thudding. The crowd goes wild. With good reason. These branded, hooded men are a clear demonstration of the confluence between graceful coordination and aggression. If our military were this coordinated and aggressive, the nation of Israel would encompass all of Dar Es Salaam and a small part of Fiji. (I've always wanted to go to Fiji. Seems like a worthwhile place to call your own.)

❧

What a show. Carla and I boom-bap-bap our way all the way back to the Grad Center.

"Ladies, wait!"

Terrell is racing our way. Carla nudges me playfully.

"You ladies want to come over to my room to celebrate?"

I look to Carla for guidance yet again. "I'm really tired," Carla says. "But you should go, Iris."

Should I? What if those black girls see me and beat me up? I guess it's worth the risk. I mean, I wanted a pool. I should swim in it.

❧

Turns out Terrell also lives in the Grad Center with several other boom bappers. Luckily they're all still at the auditorium, and we proceed to Terrell's room uninterrupted. I sit on his bed, very nervous.

"You need to relax, baby," he coos, dimming the lights and putting on some cheesy R&B. *Really* cheesy. But oddly effective.

He smooths over to the bed and leans in to kiss me. His lips are the puffiest, softest lips I have ever kissed. Wow. This is what lips are supposed to be like. (Not to diss guys with thin lips, but they feel like dried-out string beans nestled in a stubble pod, and you don't feel lip, you only feel tongue, which is usually thin and slivery in keeping with its anemic porthole.)

Terrell slowly and smoothly takes off his shirt. He slowly and smoothly takes off my shirt. In fact everything he does is smooth and slow. I get it now—sleeping with a black man is like being in your own music video. Cool! I want to turn and pout to camera and jiggle my ass a bit, but I do not.

I touch his torso like a mesmerized anatomy student. Muscles everywhere. His branding sizzles at the touch.

I can't wait to call my friends in Israel and tell them about my first night at Brown. They're not going to believe this shit.

Terrell takes off his pants and underwear. Slowly. And Smoothly. The tension is killing me. How big is he? Is he a member of the stereotype or a sad exception? While I've slept with several men, they have all been of average size. Except that one guy who was really so small that I asked him to leave the premises.

Terrell does indeed possess the largest erect member I have ever seen, heard, or read about. It is *massive*. Think two soup cans stacked on top of each other. And then some. I worry about all the blood that has to flow into his member to keep it that erect. Is he going to faint mid-act for lack of blood supply to his brain?

I wrap both hands around it. My fingers don't make it all the way around. Not even close.

With one hand Terrell lifts me up and places me beneath him. He opens a bedside cabinet where a jumbo family pack of Magnum condoms awaits.

He enters slowly. One inch at a time.

An hour later he is entirely inside me. Some of my internal organs rearrange themselves to accommodate. He undulates like a muscular snake, which I'm sure would be super pleasurable if he didn't keep whispering "baby," "fuck yeah," "oh shit," and other assorted R&B terms of endearment into my ear.

The music has grown syrupy. In fact, the singer is now crooning about the Lord and expensive champagne. Terrell keeps undulating at the same slow, smooth, sensual pace. When I'm confident my pancreas has successfully nudged its way up to my diaphragm, I whisper softly in Terrell's ear, "I want you to come, baby."

"Sure thing, babygirl."

God, having all these babies here is really creeping me out.

He does not speed up. He does not slow down. He just keeps gently grinding and undulating to the beat. Which by this time has surprisingly grown on me. I find myself grinding a little more animatedly now, shifting my hips left and right, snapping my fingers, tossing my hair this way and that while moaning, "Oh . . . baby," "Fuck yeah," and "Awwww shit!" on a rotating basis. Pretty soon we're both doing this odd horizontal dance—gyrating, grunting, singing, and moaning. We both come with a loud "Uh, huh, that's right."

I wink at the camera, and the screen fades to black.

പ

Back at cell block G, everyone's asleep, the Tex Mex queen no doubt dreaming of plantations and servitude. I am exhausted, which is good because it's keeping my nerves from focusing on the fact that classes start tomorrow. I've chosen some fun courses that don't quite warrant the ridiculously high university tuition, but they did sound enticing in the catalogue: Art History, Italian, Existential Philosophy, and something called Imagined Communities, which sounded close to my heart.

I flop onto my narrow bed, which is so hard, it boinks me right back up. Jesus Christ, it's not a bed, it's a fucking church bench. Again with the cheap choices.

I carefully re-place myself onto the plank so as not to damage any bones or muscle tissue and tuck myself in my starchy new sheets that make an unwelcoming crisp sound. I close my eyes. My mom is on the flight back to Israel right now. I wonder if she's sleeping or worrying about me. I wish I had my Jane's Addiction and Velvet Underground posters here. That huge one with the four boobs that my mom grew to love. She's so cool. Ronit got me that one. She's probably out at some bar on the beach at the moment with a bunch of our friends.

And here I am, all alone, my little body on this little bed in this little room in Providence, Rhode Island. Awww, shit.

6

BONFIRE OF THE BASEBALL CAPS

My first class starts at 9:00 a.m. in Sayles Hall. I'm ready and waiting by 7:00. It's an impressive, intimidating classical structure. I take a deep breath and massage the vibrating pit in my stomach. I'm more nervous than I thought I'd be. But who can blame me? My last classroom experience was over three years ago and involved a mousy biology teacher who spent the entire class talking about zygotes while picking banana remnants from her back teeth.

The majestic door to the building is unlocked. I push it slightly open, afraid I might be walking into some morning salon or the signing of the Declaration of Independence.

Wow. The classroom is less classroom, more Oval Office: mahogany-lined walls, plush carpeting (about time!), and a large oval wood table in the center. The professor is already here, looking even more nervous than I am. He is a teddy bear in a canary-colored sweater vest, purple bow tie, a tiny button nose, and droopy blue eyes that together give him a well-dressed sea otter look.

He introduces himself as Professor Haskins, commends me on my punctuality, and hands me a syllabus with about fifty-six books listed as required reading. He is no joke.

Other students arrive and take their seats around the table. Jesus Christ, they all look so *young*. It's like fucking Degrassi High in here. I didn't look that young when I was 18. Was it the weapons handling? The Middle Eastern air? That annoying crease I have on the upper quadrant of my forehead from worrying too much?

The crease gets deeper as I realize this class is as interesting as a rerun of *Murder, She Wrote*. Professor Haskins is droning on nervously about the inherent connection between inner cities in the Midwest and ethnic violence in Korean neighborhoods, and I am left puzzled and bored.

Luckily, my Italian class is more interesting—mainly because it involves fiery Professor Santina Sessarego, who provides the class with study aids that include a collection of figurines and pasta samples. But while learning to count and pronounce *gnocchi* correctly is all well and good, where are the intense debates and intellectual discourse promised in the pamphlet? Where is Ethan Hawke? Where is the inspiring professor who waxes poetic on life and its complexities?

Aha! Found him. Whew. In my Existential Philosophy class. He's hot, Belgian, impeccably dressed, straight, and currently running around the auditorium talking about

Kierkegaard and romantic love. I revel in two hours of mesmelust.

At the end, Professor Sexpot assigns us five books to read and announces that he will be having office hours today at 4:00 p.m. where students can talk with him one-on-one.

I am outside his door at 3:15, happy to beat the rush. So as not to look like a crazy person, I wait until 3:58 before knocking.

"Come in!" he says, his vague accent (what is Flemish, anyway?) caressing my eardrum with Belgian chocolatey mellifluousness.

We spend the entire time slot discussing Camus and Sartre. Half the time I imagine ripping off his blue blazer and having him do me on his desk. To expedite the arrival of such a glorious event, I do my best to impress him with my sharp intellect and wit. Being Belgian, he only picks up on the intellect part, but that's enough for me. (Others would say that that too would be a Belgian stretch, but they are just eurosnobs.)[9]

I return to the Grad Center feeling extremely satisfied, mentally and sexually, and decide to make my fellow prisoners some tea. The Hello Kitty dolls are practicing their trombones in Julie's room, while Mia is talking to her father about his oil surplus. I look for Carla but am told she is at track practice.

---

9 Europeans' sense of who's above whom has always puzzled me. France looks down on Italy, Italy down on Spain, Spain down on Portugal, they all laugh at Belgium, and Germany isn't even given the honor of being judged. Personally I rank by cuisine, which I guess gives one the same results.

Let me say this: I am not a runner. I don't enjoy it, and I think it stands contrary to everything evolution has taught us; now that we have transcended the standard fight-or-flight scenarios in the literal sense, our bodies need not run. At the most, a slight jog to the movie theater not to miss the previews. Anything more is abusing progress.

Mia gets off the phone and tells me she is going to the crew team party.

"I've heard of crew teams!" I yell in delight. "They were in the big fat blue guide!"

She looks at me confused. "The party's gonna be at the captain of the crew team's house," she says with gravitas. "He's a senior. And there will be lots of cute boys, too!"

"Count me in!"

❧

The crew captain's house is a two-story wood structure with a large balcony jam-packed with people. It's dark outside, so all I can make out are baseball caps. Lots of them. "Why are they all wearing baseball caps at night?" I ask, Balki-like. (I wonder what he's doing these days. He had the "Role of Flamboyant Immigrant" market totally cornered there for a while.)

Of course as I'm asking this question, Mia pulls out a baseball cap and puts it on.

The stereo inside the house is blasting some sort of horrifying indie rock that I've never heard before. There's a massive metal canister in the middle of the living room with a plastic tube coming out of it. It is surrounded by dozens of baseball-capped guys screaming, laughing, and sucking on the plastic tube.

"What's that?" Balki asks yet again.

"That's a keg. Do you want some beer?"

"No thanks, I don't like beer."

Mia approaches the tube and commences to suck. The other baseball caps cheer.

I look around, noticing the other women in the room for the first time. They look like a bunch of sluts in fleece. Their bodies are stout, muscular, and firm, their ponytails smooth and efficient, their breasts large, well-supported, and hidden under colorful sleeveless Patagonia fleece vests, their sausagey red-painted toes nestled in Tevas or flip-flops, and their sporty vaginas clearly ready to accommodate all members of every sports team on campus.

Mia wipes the beer off her chin with Reese Wither-spoon–like elegance. "That's the captain of the crew team," she says, pointing to a man at the top of the stairs, watching over the keg. He is strikingly tall, with an angular jaw and a heavenly physique. Even his baseball cap is regal.

He smiles at Mia, not even giving me a sideways glance. Maybe I'm too short and outside the range of his peripheral vision. He crosses the room to talk/make out with her. I take a seat on a ratty couch in the corner, sitting on a beer patch in the process. The monkeys around the keg are getting feistier, the tube now flailing to and fro, beer spurting everywhere, their hungry flip-flops making squishy peely sounds on the sticky hardwood floor.

Oh no. Steely Dan is playing. The Sluts in Fleece have begun to dance. Well, more like shift their hips in a robotic yet aggressive fashion. The way Cylons would dance if they had big boobs and stocky legs.

Oh no. The crew team has joined in, gyrating up against them. I can't watch. The Soul Train has crashed and burned, my friends, and this is what will remain one thousand years later after all rhythm has been abolished from the earth.

The couch beer has managed to seep through my jeans directly into my ass crack. That and the fact that none of the crew guys find me attractive begs the question—why am I still sitting here? Rejection never feels good, even if it's by someone you are repulsed by. An ego-boost is in order. I guess I could head to the black fraternity and get some ass-love (the non-penetrating kind) but that's not appealing either. Enough of this.

Mia doesn't notice me leave. With good reason. She's currently down on her knees, sucking on the tube, which is now coming out of the crew king's crotch.

The walk back to the Grad Center is a melancholy one. Images of burning baseball caps alternate with thoughts of alienation. I thought I'd feel like an American who had come back home, but now that I'm back in America, I feel like an Israeli away from home. Who was I kidding, thinking I could insert myself into this completely foreign environment and like it? And find love, to boot? I tried that in Asia, and all I got was sex. Which I guess was the goal, but it's not the goal anymore. The goal is deeper, more profound. One could say it's sex with perks. With a sense of belonging. With love. Yes, I can't deny it—love is the goal. It always has been; it has just taken different forms over the years. Right now it seems unattainable. I mean, are my only options in life to be lonely and alienated in Israel or lonely and alienated in America? Even if I *am* better off getting an amazing education here, what's all this Ivy League mental stimulation worth if my soul feels like it's in solitary confinement?

☙

Carla is sitting on the floor rubbing her divine calves when I enter. Long day at practice, she tells me, adding that she's training for the Olympics. I tell her I'm training for depression.

She rushes over and hugs me so hard that my vertebrae squeal. Her sudden compassion is jarring and comforting all at once. I launch into an "America feels like a foreign land" monologue. Carla listens intently. *Really* listens. I don't think I've ever experienced a real listener before. Who would have thought being truly heard is so fantastic?

"You should hang out with the European students!" she finally declares. "I'm sure they feel exactly the way you do. I think there's a party at their dorm tomorrow!"

The Euros. I had not considered myself a potential member of that group, maybe because Israel is not part of Europe. Israelis would like to *think* of our/themselves as part of Europe (except during the World Cup trials), but no matter how hard we try, we remain in the Middle East, much to the dismay of our neighbors. Nevertheless, I'm encouraged by Carla's suggestion and go to bed with some hope in my cockles.

℘

That night I am awakened by a bang on the wall from Plain Yogurt's room. Then a one-minute pause. Then another bang. Old pipes?

I put my ear up to the wall and hear the bed creaking. Plain Yogurt is banging! Or getting banged, whatever the less offensive term is. Her man is obviously a slow lover—the bangs are thirty seconds apart. And hard. Super hard. Since we don't have headboards, that could only be her head banging into the wall. I hope she's wearing a helmet. God why am I such a light sleeper, this is going to be a nightmare. Oh, wait, he's going faster now, her head's really taking a beating. Jesus, that can't be fun.

Ooh, three quick bangs.

Then silence.

Wow, not exactly a trooper. Poor girl. Lucky me. Good night.

7

IBITHA

The Euros are housed in a building called Buxton Hall, right off the Frat Quad. No wonder they feel out of touch. I can't wait to meet my well-gelled brethren and party the night away. Will they be the jeans-hiked-up-to-their-nipples, powder-blue-sweater-tied-over-their-shoulder types or the Drakkar Noired Ibiza megamixers?

They are neither. To my relief, I enter Buxton Hall to find the latest Radiohead track blasting and a cornucopia of people from all over the globe, with neither a baseball cap nor fleshy tanned calf in sight! Within minutes, I meet students from Paris, La Paz, Athens, Johannesburg, Lagos, and Seoul. They are a remarkably cohesive group, considering that the only thing they have in common is that they are non-American. I guess that's as good a bonding factor as any.

The *internacionals* are happy to include me in their discussion lamenting American culture. I contribute eagerly, for here are people who understand my pain. I tell them about the crew party and how I sat on some beer. They cringe. I tell them how I almost got killed by four black women at a step show. They have no idea what I'm talking about but nod earnestly anyway.

Ooh! The music has gone salsa! The Latin contingent cheers, and everyone pairs off and starts dancing. Temi, a tall muscular Nigerian with zesty mini-dreads grabs me and starts to meringue. He pulls me close—way closer than the other couples are dancing—and within seconds I feel his manhood engorged. No matter how hard I try to create some distance between my crotch and his Afrocock, he pushes up against me, all the while moving his hips in a ridiculously wavy fashion, whispering in a heavy African French accent, "There must be no air between us."

I finally manage to disengage and pass him off to a Greek chick named Filo Dough or something and continue to mingle.

As I munch on some carrots and take in the frenzy, a handsome olive-skinned guy approaches me. He's from Amman.

"You're from Jordan? Oh my GOD! I'm from ISRAEL!" I exclaim, excited about the prospect of promoting the peace process over veggie sticks. "Where do you live?" I ask, as if I were well versed on Amman's hip neighborhoods.

"The Royal Palace."

I wait for the rim shot, but he's not kidding. The guy is a fucking prince. Literally. I suddenly notice his fine threads. Subtle but expensive. I look at the other students. Their threads are fine too. I soon discover that the Bolivian is the president's son, Filo Dough hails from a shipping magnate family, and the Nigerian, well, he's just creepy and gets easily aroused. These guys are rich, but not rich like that kid in my high school who had a basketball court in his backyard. I'm talking Royal-fucking-Palace rich. Now that's a bonding factor.

I've never been around such wealth. I grew up in a massive project-like building in an Israeli ghetto in the Bronx and then moved to a slightly nicer project-like building in the Israeli ghetto of Israel.[10]

The Bronx ghetto was a massive red brick compound called Skyview. Our small apartment was on the twentieth floor and had both a spectacular view of New Jersey and puke-green carpeting in every room. The Skyview pool reeked of aftershave and backgammon, and most of the tenants were Israelis searching for the American dream.

My mom's best friend, Naama Razin, lived in 5E. She had left the isolated life of the kibbutz for a bigger and better one in New York City. Naama was a painter. Most of her paintings depicted large heads of lettuce and tits. And the occasional meat grinder.

Naama and her handsome husband Ruben had four children. Their youngest, Dina, was my best friend. Many a happy year did little Dina and I spend in the Israeli ghetto of Skyview, leaping from her apartment to mine, playing

---

10 Sure, sometimes I'd marvel at the really hot rich girls in my class, like Karine, and wonder why good looks and rich parents often went hand in hand. Karine's dad was a sexy former soccer player who owned a bra factory. These days, however, the rich guys are dorky start-up millionaires who, despite their hot, money-hungry wives, are just ugly Internet geeks and inevitably have mediocre-looking offspring.

Malibu Barbie, Operation, Monopoly, Risk, and every other board game manufactured in the '80s.

One day, I ran down to the Razins' apartment only to find the door open and moving boxes everywhere. Dina was crying. Naama was running around packing up her lettuce tits. "My dad suddenly made a lot of money," she said to me. "So we are moving to Manhattan."

We never found out how Dina's dad made all that Manhattan money, but a week later the Razins moved into a palatial duplex overlooking Central Park—the kind of duplex that has Madonna as your neighbor, gold leafing along the hallways, and a tubby Puerto Rican who presses the elevator buttons for you.

It was right after Dina moved on up that my parents' marriage began to disintegrate in a public fashion. The Razins' fat pad in the city became our asylum, a safe haven to which my mother and I would flee every weekend from our misery at home. Those weekends usually consisted of my mother following Naama around the Upper West Side as she bought designer clothes and expensive cakes while Dina and I stayed at home eating coffee Häagen-Dazs and watching Monty Python flicks on HBO.

Apparently marital problems are contagious because our beloved safe haven soon became a marital disaster zone as well, and Dina and I watched as *her* parents' marriage fell apart and my mom and I were forced to return to our relative shithole and actually deal with our own emotional muck and mire.

❧

The Euros prove to be a lovely bunch and I begin to hang out with them on a regular basis.

It's nice being exposed to such a wide human array of colors and backgrounds, like Carlos from Ecuador who favors tight jeans that outline his testicles, the French girls Audrey and Juliette who have constantly hard nipples and smoke a lot, and hybrids like Lucy (half Asian, half British) who hails from Hong Kong and has a movie theater in her basement back home.

Carlos takes a particular liking to me and invites me to numerous dinners at his house that involve lots of wine and dancing by the fireplace with his Colombian comrades.[11] He even nurses me back to health after I get my wisdom teeth pulled out. I try to want him, but I can't get over the urge to pull his pants away from his balls. He also has a disturbing tendency to stare at me lovingly without blinking. (That's not fear of intimacy on my part, that's fear of weirdness, right?)

"Why won't you kiss me?" Carlos asks me on his fifth attempt in a week to get some action.

"My wisdom teeth still hurt," I reply.

"But they took them out three weeks ago," he says, confused.

"It's like a phantom limb; they're gone, but the pain of their absence remains."

---

11 Since the only other Ecuadorian is a pudgy professor in the Biomechanical Engineering Department who can't dance, Carlos was forced to make friends with the Colombians.

Carlos finally accepts that I'm not attracted to him, agrees to be my BFF, and promptly makes the moves on Lucy, who by now annoys the fuck out of me. Imagine a high-pitched voice that crackles at random intervals, super-human yoga skills, and incessant talk about that damn movie theater in her basement.

Being the honest BFF-y soul that I am, I tell Carlos that Lucy drives me insane, that her voice sounds like a bird in heat, that the thing she does with her legs over her head is creepy, and that they are not right for each other. So he breaks up with her. Which I have to admit makes me happy. Until he tells me he's thrilled that we can now be together.

"What?"

"That's why you told me to break up with Lucy, because you wanted to be with me."

"No, because she was really annoying."

"You mean you don't want to be with me?"

"Well, not romantically, no . . . I thought we were best fr—"

Carlos glares down at me (he's tall) with such shock and hate that I fear for my life. He's Latin; who's to say he won't kill me in the heat of passion? That's par for the course for these constricted testicle guys.

"I'm sorry for the misunderstanding, Carlos, I—"

Carlos lifts his hand. "Don't ever speak to me again. Don't ever come *near* me again, and don't ever, *ever*, speak my name in public."

That last part confuses me, but I think it best to not ask for clarification. I feel horrible for hurting Carlos's feelings but am also eager for him to storm off already because he's just standing there staring at me without blinking.

Needless to say, that was the end of our friendship, and I am forced to turn to other Euros for companionship, like Koo Yim, a six-foot-tall lithe Korean girl who invites me to take a day trip to Boston to go shopping with her. Finally some girl stuff! And with a cool Asian chick! Sweet!

Koo Yim picks me up in a convertible of German origin and whisks us off to Boston on the most efficient and ridiculous spendathon I've ever witnessed; $3,000 in less than two hours, all on interchangeable items of black clothing.

I am too shocked to be jealous. I could never spend that much money on clothing, even if I had it. The guilt would kill me. Not over the money part, or the ridiculousness of spending that much on black cotton part—just the buying nice things for oneself part. My mother taught me that spending money on oneself is *baaaad*, whereas spending money on other people is *gooood*. My mother, you see, will never buy anything for herself but doesn't step a foot in someone else's house without a generous gift in hand. She has ingrained that ethic deep inside me. As a result, we both have very appreciative friends and a very meager wardrobe.

I do end up buying a ridiculously expensive pair of socks at Armani on Newbury Street and follow leggy Koo Koo back to her convertible to unload the merchandise before we drive off to meet eight more Korean students for dinner at some chi-chi restaurant.

The Korean crew are all very nice and make an effort to speak English every fourteen minutes. The food too is amazing and keeps coming in large amounts and odd textures, odder than anything I sampled in Asia on my sex tour a year ago.

The check finally arrives. The head Korean announces, "Okay, everybody, that's 120 bucks a piece." They all pull out cash from their wallets.

I turn pink. Then green. Then red.

For Chrissake, I only had two dumplings and a glass of water for a total of $8.99! But do I want to be that annoying person at the table that starts nitpicking over who ate what, haggling over a dollar here or a dollar there?? Then again, this is $120. That I don't have.

Kimchee pulls out a wad of cash from her wallet and slaps it on the table.

"This is for both of us," she says to the table. She smiles at me. I want to die. The Koreans are all looking at me—the poor Israeli with no shopping bags. Shit. They must think I'm cheap. And now they're gonna think all Jews are cheap, which couldn't be farther from the truth. (My friends in Israel have no regard for money whatsoever—pathologically so.) But honestly, what the fuck are these kids doing ordering a $120 meal? They're 19 years old! Forget that, what are they doing spending thousands of dollars in a single day?

I suddenly feel sick to my stomach and hunger for my puny little dorm room and tea with Carla. I'm relieved when Koo Yim tells everyone she is too shopped-out to go for some post-dinner clubbing with the other Koreans, and she drives me back to my warm and cozy prison cell before zipping back to her fancy off-campus condo.

❧

To my dismay, Carla's not at home, Plain Yogurt is getting thwacked double time, and the Hello Kitties are spooning their violins. I tiptoe into my room and start to cry; a deep penetrating sense of sadness, loneliness, helplessness, uselessness, and debilitating worthlessness. I'm afraid I'm not going to make it through this whole Brown experience. Something's gotta give.

8

SOAP

I am relieved to realize there's still one clique left on campus that I haven't tapped into yet, and I'm praying to the Almighty they are more up my alley. Neither tube-sucking cap-happy jocks or sushi-snorting spend-happy Euros, this group lives in a commune, which, being on an Ivy League campus, is not some flowery teepee mud hut but a massive three-story Victorian house with a front porch, rocking chairs, and good vibes. They call it a co-op, and they share everything—food, responsibilities, bodily fluids, and love. Lots and lots of love. These people sound simple and endearing, and I know that they will find a place in their hearts for a lost soul like me and envelop me in their patchouli-smelling ponchos.

These hippies, if you will, like to ring in the school year with a Naked Party, which is exactly what it sounds like—a bunch of naked people hanging out with everything hanging out, sans worries or self-consciousness or judgment. Just what I need to get better again.

Not to disappoint the masses, but I don't plan on getting naked at this party. I know they will understand. With time, I will learn their ways and feel comfortable enough to have them see my pubic area while making breakfast.[12]

For regulatory reasons, the hippies hanging on the front porch are partially clothed. The men are barefoot, chubby, and have full-on Amishy beards, some of which have cottage cheese remnants or gummy bears nestled within. The women are all equally plump, with long curly flowy hair, long peasant skirts, and drippy smiles. There is no doubt in my mind that I do NOT want to see any of these people naked. Ever.

Come on, woman. That's the judgmental bitch in you talking. You're not exactly Heidi Klum. You're five-foot-fucking-four-inches tall, have cellulite on your left thigh, and your calf muscles are as toned as a milkshake, so get over yourself and walk into that big house and make some naked friends.

I walk up the stairs. The butter churners smile at me through their beards. I smile back as I push open the front door. BAM! A wave of hot air reeking of sweat, human foot, and ass crack hits me like a vegan garlic tsunami. Before my retinas are hit with the corresponding image, I shut the door and rush back down the stairs, right past this cute boy with wispy long hair and a violin case who laughs at the horrified look on my face. His exterior is relatively clean and his beard food-free, so I happily stop and smile. His name is Brodie, and his eyelids are locked at stoner half-mast.

---

12 There is a very oily strip joint in Providence that advertises a brunch special called Legs 'n' Eggs, which I can only assume involves eating a rubbery omelet while a stripper shakes her wares over your plate. Appetizing.

"Too intense for you, huh," Brodie says, enveloping me in warm love.

"Yeah."

"These will help." He pulls out a bag of mushrooms and offers me some. I tell him I am afraid of taking mind-altering drugs not only because of my brother's condition but also because I am terrified of losing control.

"That's exactly why you should take them," he says, "to confront your fears."

"That makes sense, and also sounds like horrible advice," I reply. I'm confused as to what to do at this juncture, but I really want to sleep with this guy so maybe I should just shut up and listen to him.

"And besides," Brodie continues, "Shrooms are natural."

I remind Brodie that some of the most potent poisons are also found in nature and that the whole "natural shit can't hurt you" argument doesn't fly. He seems unfazed by this logic and soothingly describes the wonderful sensations fungi can offer, including a vast array of colors, smells, and vibrations. I tell Brodie my vibratory experiences have been limited to my electronic toothbrush and Steve, my vibrator. Steve was shaped like a little rabbit. I used him so much his ears burned off and I had to throw him away. I also tell Brodie that despite his slightly moldy exterior I find him extremely attractive and suggest we go back to my place and explore each other's bodies.

To avoid any unpleasant discoveries during intercourse, I first drag Brodie to the shower and give him a full cavity scrub down. I learn then that marijuana odor is subdermal and extremely resistant to soap and boiling water. But I get

Brodie clean enough for copulation and we happily retire to the pleasure center to have some hippie fun.

Hippie fun turns into what Americans term "We are dating," and over the next week Brodie teaches me what it's like to have a beard exfoliate one's labia, what a wheatgrass burp smells like, and how to find bliss in relaxation. Well, everything but that last part. Brodie keeps telling me I'm "too intense" and "I worry too much." I worry he's going to leave me. I want to be more like him, I really do—I want to shroom my neuroses out of body, fuck the fear out of it, and learn to love tofu, but I'm scared.

But it's time to stop being scared. Brodie has left a large bag of mushrooms on my desk, and I'm going to surprise him and take them, and the next time he sees me I'm going to be all blissed out and talk to him about the mind portal and greater consciousness and fuchsia clouds and shit, and we will love each other forever.

I suddenly recall that Elena, a girl who lives in the cell block downstairs, mentioned that she had wanted to try shrooms. I've always liked Elena. The daughter of a rich physician, she is half WASP and half Dominican, a rare combination that has blessed her with blonde hair, a dark complexion, and a great sense of edgy humor. Elena is thrilled to experiment with hallucinogens and rushes over to begin the journey.

I recall Brodie telling me he always eats the entire stash with peanut butter. Unfortunately the only kind of peanut butter I have is super chunky, and in our drug-hungry, shove-the-shrooms-down-our-throats frenzy we almost choke in the process.

Elena and I head toward a little park by the Grad Center and wait for the effects to hit. When they do, they hit *hard*. The first ten minutes involve shiny sidewalk diamonds, worm-oozing trees, and a talking moon. We are in psychedelic heaven.

At minute eleven, Elena freaks out.

"We are going to die." She starts chanting nervously. "We are going to DIE!"

How could the freakout begin so fucking soon? Forget that—how could I pick the one person on this entire campus who would freak out? Fuck, we have eight hours to go of this insanity.

"Take me to my room!" she demands, breathing erratically.

I oblige immediately, hoping to nip this in the bud. We enter the stairwell and begin to climb toward the first floor. Considering how leaden our legs are, we might as well be climbing Kilimanjaro. I point to some diamonds oozing out of the banister, but freakazoid's not having it.

The moment we enter her room, she leaps onto her bed and buries her face in the pillow. "We're going to die," she announces yet again.

I begin to sweat, the tiny room closing in on me fast. "Elena, let's go back outside. It's not good to stay inside, we need fresh air."

Elena doesn't respond. I shake her annoyingly thin body. She's fading. I shake her some more, but she has fallen into panic-induced slumber.

I stumble upstairs to my room, wondering if I should try and sleep it off as well. I plop onto my bed, somehow exhausted. Elena had the right idea—ten minutes of intense shrooming and then a relaxing sleep to recuperate. I close my eyes.

And then the scary images begin. Horrible images, traumatizing, repulsive images. Of me tango dancing with a tomato. An aggressive tomato that throws me into a large bowl of Caesar dressing. No lettuce, just Caesar dressing. Pure, unadulterated Caesar dressing that coats my entire being—heart, mind, and soul—trapping me in its creamy grasp. I start to choke and sweat, the visceral sensation of death by salad overpowering my remaining sense of sanity. Fear sets in. Elena was right. We are going to die.

I force my rubbery body off the bed and, like a rag doll, pray to the only deity available: the large Navajo rug hanging on my wall.

"You are the Carpet God," I say. "Please make these shrooms wear off soon before my brain melts."

The Carpet God pulls out a small Peruvian flute and asks me to purchase his latest CD.

I stumble back outside and roam the streets in search of calming fresh air. It's already three in the morning, and this part of Providence is a shady place. I decide to proceed no further and plop down on a comforting patch of grass alongside the road, thrusting my hands into the mud, or—as it's more accurately called—dog shit.

For some reason, this doesn't faze me, and I start to make tiny shit sculptures. I make a Shit King, and a Shit Queen with a beautiful crown on her shit head. I watch as Shit King kisses Shit Queen softly on her shit lips. They make shit babies that dance around the shit castle doing shit dances.

Dog shit is not made for long term sculpture, however, and by the time the Shit King fucks the Shit Queen on the shit futon, the shit village is nothing but a splattery mess, and my shit panic sets in again.

I need to find Brodie. He'll know what to do. He'll guide me. He'll bring me to that happy place he was describing, where everything smells like marzipan and honeysuckle, and I will bathe in existential epiphanies.

I ring Brodie's buzzer with my least shitty finger.

"I'll be right down, Iris, hang in there," he tells me in his soothing voice.

Forty minutes and several tulip-shaped joints later Brodie ambles down the stairs. He opens the door with grace and aplomb.[13]

"Guide me, Brodie. I'm losing it."

He looks at me intently. "Just feel the love, Iris. Feel the love."

I look at him. He's serious.

"Feel the love?" I cry. *Feel the love?* How am I supposed to feel the fucking love? I'm covered in dog shit! I just prayed to a textile! I have no fucking love to feel!!

I wanna wipe my fecal fingers over his glassy eyeballs. But my hands are too fucking heavy, and they end up resting awkwardly on my right shoulder before they can make it up to his face.

---

13 I used to think aplomb meant a really productive bowel movement. It should.

Brodie pops a papal kiss on the one tiny clean patch of my forehead and wanders back up the stairs, leaving me staring at my confused and shit-stained reflection in the glass door. It looks like a flying horse took a dump on me. It sure feels like it.

❧

Brodie and I try to hang out a few more times, but my inability to feel the love really gets to him, and his ability to overlove gets to me (I discover that I am just one of many women whose labia are currently being exfoliated by the Brodester), and we part ways amicably.

Doesn't change the fact that I'm depressed, though. The sad reality is, I have nowhere else to turn, nowhere to go. No clique has been left unturned (I spared you the boring ones). Hell, I even tried to be Asian for a day. All that is left at this juncture is to kill myself and summarize my anthropological findings in chart form for your referencing convenience. Let's recap.

Official Ivy League Clique Breakdown

In no particular order/degree of my alienability. Note that many students do not fall under one particular category, i.e. black students, Jewish students, and generic white students (who are irrelevant to society anyway). Hence, they are not included in this list.

- **The Internationals:** Extremely wealthy Europeans, Africans, Arabs (only if they were educated in London

---

first), and Latin Americans (only if they own apartments in Miami). Make frequent trips to Boston for shopping sprees and clubbing. Good on the dance floor. Have come to America to major in economics, proceed to business school, and promptly return to rule home country.

- **The Frat Boys:** Beefy, infantile, own at least seven baseball caps, constantly reek of beer, tube socks, and Old Spice deodorant.

- **The Jocks:** Subspecies of Frat Boys. Contain all of the above characteristics but are also sporty and dim. Note: not all Frat Boys are in good enough shape to be Jocks, but almost all Jocks are Frat Boys.

- **The Maya Angelou/Amiri Baraka African-Americans:** Subgroup of black students who are particularly passionate about their African heritage. Intelligently angry when provoked. And when not provoked.

- **The Vegan Commie Hippies:** Concentrated in co-ops that involve shared food, communal living, and no soap. Ingest an exorbitant amount of mushrooms, lack all coordination, and dance like rag-dolls. Girls are on the chubbier side and favor long skirts and tank tops that barely contain their juggie breasts and massive nipples that range in the four- to six-inch radius range. Boys sport unruly dreadlocks and bushy beards that usually contain remnants of tofu chunks prepared at the co-op with the other nonbathers.

- **The Asian Pre-Meds:** Brilliant, wiry, über-motivated wannabe doctors who are following in mama and papa's footsteps. Genitalia minimal. For both sexes.

- **The New Yorkers:** Sons and daughters of wealthy intellectuals from Manhattan. Have been groomed for Ivy League education since they were in the womb. Attended prep schools with odd names like Choate and Exeter. Pretentious, snooty, and attractive. Have been doing cocaine since the ninth grade.

- **The Celeb Offspring:** Children of famous people, a cornucopia of both dumb and smart youth, some more blessed with their parents' outward genetics than others (or cursed, depending on the parent).

- **The Legacy Tots:** Students whose parents, grandparents, and/or great-grandparents went to the school. Insecure that they are smart enough to have been admitted. Buildings are named after their ancestors.

- **The Urban Hipsters:** Fans of Wu Tang Clan. Know the backstreets of Baltimore. Use all drugs in equal measure. Make films and street art. Impressive T-shirt collection.

9

THE BULB IS DIM

The University Psychological Services Department refers me to a Dr. Wallace Kaufman, whose salvatorium is located on Hope Street in a grand, baby blue colonial house with lavender trim. I arrive an hour early to our scheduled appointment and enter the house with the furtive nature typical of a person who does not want to be discovered as mentally vulnerable and in search of outside assistance.

The foyer is dark and smells of mold and desperation. I walk up the creaky stairs, my heart pounding, and find a large mahogany door and a small light switch with a small plaque underneath that reads:

PLEASE TURN SWITCH ON
TO ANNOUNCE ARRIVAL

What if I touch it and neon lights reading "Fucked-up Jew Girl" begin blazing, and Jamiroquai pops out and does that really cool weird dance that he does? I guess that's just a risk I have to take. So I flip the switch, then sit on a slithery yet sturdy maroon leather chair and wait for something life-changing to happen.

The heavy wood door opens and a rotund, egg-shaped man in a gray sweater, square glasses, and sweet smile appears. "You must be Iris!" he says, pronouncing it per-fectly. Wow, he actually listened to the way I said it on his voice mail. I love this man already!

His office smells a lot less like mold and desperation and more like hope and expensive air freshener. I ease into a chair opposite his and grin nervously.

"So why are you here, Iris?" he asks, cocking his head gently to the left.

And so it begins.

The Therapeutic Process
(In Sixteen Easy Steps)

Step 1: Introductory trust-building phase. Getting com-fortable with strange man. General, nonpainful question-ing. Some awkward laughter.

Step 2: Griping, moaning, and bitching. Dr. Kaufman con-firms my theory that my feeling of alienation is due to the fact that I'm older and not connected logically or organi-cally to any clique on campus.

Step 3: Slight dabbling into childhood memories. Release of one to three tears.

Step 4: First traumatic memory recall. Intense weeping, several nose blows, loving smile, encouragement to go deeper.

Step 5: Deeper trauma recall. Anger, frustration, hopelessness. Full box of Kleenex.

Step 6: Even deeper trauma recall. More anger, frustration, hopelessness. Therapist plants seed that my parents are horrible people. This thought is comforting, as there is a reason for my madness.

Step 7: New traumatic memories that the body so safely concealed for logical reasons are suddenly unleashed. Two and a half boxes blown. Dr. Kaufman realizes that, contrary to what he initially thought, my alienation is actually due to *my* being fucked up and nothing to do with the outside world.

Step 8: Discovery that my parents are to blame for ALL my dysfunctional behaviors, including my inability to do simple math equations in my head and my intolerance for lactose. Hatred of parents bubbles to the surface.

Step 9: Hatred of parents erupts with force. I feel empowered, justified, legitimate.

Step 10: Hatred of parents peaks. Therapist encourages me to confront parents verbally over their psychologically criminal behaviors.

Step 11: Several phone calls to parents to communicate the horrors they've done are met on their part with a frustrating combination of confusion, resentment, anger, and nonchalance.

Step 12: Therapist deplores parents for behavior in Step 11, which further amplifies Steps 9 and 10 and commences a vicious cycle that gets worse every week.

Step 13: Therapist reveals to me that this is by far the worst childhood-divorce story he's heard in his career as a therapist. I feel special for a moment and then realize I'd rather not feel special for that particular reason.

Step 14: I reveal to therapist that I'm actually a lot more depressed than I was when we started seeing each other. He tells me it's part of the process, and would I like some anti-depressants, perchance? I decline and inquire as to when the helpful, feel-better, get-rid-of-issues part starts. He apologizes and says our time is up for the day.

Step 15: I am unable to function outside the therapist's office. My parents have ceased to speak to me. I am angry at the world and see no help in sight.

Step 16: I tell Dr. Kaufman that I think I should stop therapy. He says he's feeling equally depressed from our sessions and couldn't agree more. We part ways. He says if I ever want to come in and recall more traumas, he is always here for me. He gives me a warm hug and shows me the door.

10

OUTTA HERE LIKE VLADIMIR

Understanding how horrible my childhood was has done nothing but remind me of how horrible my childhood was. If only I could turn back time to when I thought I was normal and everyone else was a freak. It's me. I'm the problem. And the problem is me. Which means my depression is incurable unless I change me. How the hell am I supposed to do that? I'm too depressed to change. Isn't that why I went into therapy in the first place?

But I am not a victim. I. Am. Not. A. Victim. I'm a fighter. I've fought my whole life, and I will keep fighting. I will fight this depression on my own. Forget therapy. Forget vegetable drugs. Forget trying to connect with these ridiculous people with their childlike groups and clans. The academic year has come to a close, and I have three months of summer vacation ahead of me, and I'm going to get out of here. But go where?

I can't go back home to Israel. Israel means Ima drowning us both in pity and my friends egging to hear stories of me getting pleasured atop a stack of Kierkegaard readers. There's only one real option that can offer any comfort: a trip. To South America.

Why South America? Because that's where Israelis go after the army if they don't go to Asia. And I've already been to Asia. And South America is closer to America than Asia. And it's really the same thing as Asia, only with regime changes, kidnappings, bus hijackings, and other assorted activities that will no doubt take my mind off my current state of lumpitude and engulf me with my beloved kinsmen—only not in their native environment. Because if you're going to feel like an alien, you might as well go where everyone else feels like an alien too. And have some fun in the process.

But where does an alien get funds for such a journey, considering the only job alien has had time for in the past year was getting paid $10 an hour to slice lunch meat in the university cafeteria on Wednesdays and Saturdays?

❧

Ring, ring.

"Hello?"

"Hey, Pop, it's me."

"Irischuni!"

"I want to start by saying that I take back everything I said about me hating you for everything you've done to me in the last fifteen years and that I love you very much and think you're great."

"Oh, well I'm glad to hear we've moved past that non-sense. How are classes?"

"Great. Everything is great. Can I ask you a question?"

"Of course."

"I need my bat mitzvah money."

"That's not a question."

"Sorry, I guess it was a statement. I just recall that I received quite a bit of money for my bat mitzvah ten years ago that you so kindly and responsibly deposited in a bank account for me, and I want to cash it in."

"It wasn't just money, Iris. You also received that beautiful Gucci watch from my boss as a token of appreciation for my many years of service."

"That turned out to be a fake, Dad, remember?"

"It was not a fake!"

"Yeah, Dad, remember—we had to get the battery replaced, and the watch guy told us it was a cheap fake from Chinatown."

"I don't remember that . . . In any case, what do you need the money for, Iris?"

"I'm going to South America."

Silence.

"Pop, are you there?"

"Yes, I'm here . . . That money was meant for something responsible."

"What's more responsible than a trip to South America? Okay, I'm sure there are a lot of things more responsible than a trip, but I don't think a trip is *irresponsible*, right?"

"Why do you need to go to South America?"

"Come on, Pop, you've traveled all over the world. Don't you want your daughter to see the world too?"

"You just came back from six months in Asia!"

"That was a year ago."

"Pop?"

"Yes."

"That was a year ago."

"How much do you need?"

"How much is in there?"

"$4,000."

"Okay, great."

"Where do you plan on going?"

"Well, I thought I would start with Uncle Shmulike in Peru."

"You want to see your uncle?"

"Yes."

"You hate your uncle."

"I hated him when he lived in Tel Aviv. I don't hate him now that he lives in Peru."

"That's wonderful. He'd be so happy to see you!"

"Pop, I also thought you could recommend some other destinations since you know South America so well. You are such an accomplished and well-traveled man."

"Well, yes, you are correct, I know Latin America like the back of my hand."

"Great, Pop, well send me a detailed itinerary and my check for $4,000, and I will be on my way!"

"Great, I'm so happy you're going!"

"South America was such a great idea, Pop. I cannot thank you enough! I'm so happy we spoke!"

"Well, traveling is the essence of life, Irischuni. It's part of learning!"

"Yes, it is. Okay, Pop, I gotta go. Love you!"

"Love you too!"

Click.

☙

Who would have thought my bat mitzvah would have such a festive payoff ten years later? I'd written off that grandiose event as just another awkward chapter in my discombobulated childhood at the yeshiva, which involved constantly trying to hide the fact that I was leading a double life as an Orthodox Jewish girl by day and a baconizing secularist by night. If my parents who put me in that situation in the first place would have actually been cooperative in helping me keep up this charade, allowing me the peer acceptance/social sanity so crucial to a young girl, there wouldn't have been a problem. But they were not.

On the contrary. They did crazy shit to embarrass me and blow my cover on purpose. Like the time my mom decided to roll up RIGHT in front of the Orthodox shul in her beat-up blue Ford Torino ON THE SABBATH and holler my name at the top of her lungs until I came out and got in the car with her.[14] And her consequent attempt to make it up to me by organizing a party for my classmates that, according to her, "would be so much fun, the other kids will forget they ever saw you entering a vehicle on Shabbat!"

---

14 For those not Hebraically informed, driving a car is strictly prohibited on the Sabbath, and rolling up in a beat-up blue Torino to pick up your daughter, who everyone thinks is Orthodox, is equivalent to licking a golden calf while uncircumsizing your son.

To her credit, she did try to do good on that one, even making the effort to order kosher pizza for the event and ensuring that all the snacks had an OU label (the Orthodox seal of approval) on the package. For a while, it seemed like the party did alleviate all suspicions that the Bahrs were not devout Jews. That is, until semi-diabetic Esther Konigsberg went into the kitchen to get a glass of water and noticed that the Bahrs did not have two separate sinks for milk and meat, which meant the Bahrs were not kosher, which meant that the plates they were eating the kosher pizza on were not kosher either, which meant the kids had to call the rabbi immediately, and leave the Bahrs' house before Satan leapt out of the sink and shoved the pizza slices down their throats, dooming them to pepperoni hell for all eternity.

My bat mitzvah was my last bastion of redemption. And I was not going to let my parents mess it up. I told them in no uncertain terms: It was going to be an Orthodox event in an Orthodox hall with an Orthodox band and a super kosher Orthodox kitchen with nine sinks.

Mama and Papa Bahr complied with my demands, down to the klezmer band from Boro Park. I was the star of the appropriately observant night and couldn't be happier. For the first time in a long while, I felt safe and in control of my surroundings, which is what I desperately needed. (Their ugly divorce proceedings were at peak level, as was my anxiety and propensity to burst out in tears at any given moment.) The men were dancing the *Hora* in one circle, the women were dancing the *Hora* in a separate circle, and everyone was having an appropriately fantastic Orthodox time.

And then, out of the corner of my eye, I spotted my parents walking across the dance floor toward the band. My stomach dropped. Why were my parents approaching the band? I broke off from the *Hora* circle and raced over.

"Ima, what do you need from the band?" I asked as my father talked to the clarinet player.

"We have a song request," she replied innocently.

"Song request?"—*we?*—"Why do you need to request a song? The band has their whole Orthodox playlist already prepared!"

"Your father and I want to dance."

"What? Why would you want to dance? You can't stand each other!"

"Nobody has to know that. Everyone thinks we're still happily married."

I ignored the absurd part of her comment and focused on the emergency at hand. "But you can't dance!"

"Why not?"

"Because men are not supposed to dance with women in public, Ima!"

"That's silly, Iris."

The sweat on my vulnerable brow started to bead. The Orthodox valve in my heart began to flutter uncontrollably.

"Ima, you promised this would be Orthodox. I can't have you and Aba dancing in front of everyone!"

But it was too late. The band launched into a very odd klezmer rendition of "Strangers in the Night." The *Hora* circles paused, confused, and dispersed to the perimeter as, to my horror, my father, a forced smile pasted on his face, took my mother, an even more forced smile pasted on her face, by the hand and led her to the center of the dance floor, where they commenced to dance with each other. My classmates looked away, ashamed.

Me? I spent the entire song staring at the clarinet player with such possessed rage that the minute the song was finished he raced to the bathroom to wipe the pee stain off the inner thigh of his pants. Poor guy. Had I known then that the proceeds of said event would be saving my ass now, I wouldn't have stared so hard.

11
PASTRAMI ON RYE

My oldest, bestest friend in the world is a girl named Talia. Well, maybe she's not my *oldest* friend. That would be Dina, but she put an abrupt end to our friendship ten years ago when she left society to become a park ranger in the Yukon, and my oldest-oldest friends back from my yeshiva days all moved to the West Bank to have fourteen children and live in illegal outposts that are "obstructing the peace process."

Talia and I met on my first day of school in Israel, no doubt one of the scariest days of my life. There I was, a sweet, young American girl, thrust into a group of abrasively honest Israeli eighth graders who made fun of my lame Hebrew and the heavy American accent that accompanied that lame Hebrew. Not to mention my dykie haircut and small boobs.

Talia too had a dykie haircut that was worse than mine, mainly because her brown hair was super thick and unruly, giving her a "wild dykebeast in the forest" look. She had a bumpy nose and pesto-colored eyes that slanted slightly upward, hinting of ancient Asian ancestry or her mother's possible one-time liaison with the local Acupuncturist. She had very thin legs, absolutely no ass, and huge, magnificent breasts, the kind that lead me to believe God was more of a horndog than a stickler for proportions.

Talia had just moved back to Israel after eight years in America. She therefore knew my pain. She spoke my language. She liked my dykie haircut. She let me eat some of her sandwich. (My mother had a strong aversion to making sandwiches and gave me money every day to buy an egg sandwich from the sketchy Iraqi guy who hovered right outside the school gates wearing a stained yellow sweatshirt and acid wash jeans.)

I thought speaking English with Talia instead of lame Hebrew would alleviate the teasing by the other kids. Not the case. Speaking English was viewed as showing off (I should have moved to France instead) and caused much resentment among the Israeli kids, who were still learning their English active verbs from an unattractive South African woman who looked like a skeletal Cousin It. And so most of the time Talia and I found ourselves sitting together in the corner, talking about the other kids while they talked about us.

Talia's mother was a calm, cool, and collected blonde therapist, and her daughter came out accordingly; Talia was never one to worry or over-emote, which is why I always felt slightly too emotional and overwrought when I was with her. We did always have a great time together, though, listening to Bryan Adams records, making goofy mix tapes of us rapping, comparing nipple sizes, and the like.

Talia is somewhat surprised to hear from me after being incommunicado for the last eight months but is thrilled to hear of my South American offer. I don't share with her the real reason I need this trip and her familiar companionship—how I don't feel like getting out of bed in the morning, how I feel like a five-year-old reliving all the traumas I so bravely weathered as a child but ironically feel ill-equipped to handle as an adult, etc. I just ask her if she wants to go to South America for three months, and she says yes.

I suggest we start in Peru at my Uncle Shmulike's place, and Talia says that sounds "great." (She rarely says great, so I tend to believe her when she does, even though her delivery is always even-keeled and subdued.) We don't discuss anything beyond that—just a starting point, an end date, and all possibilities in between. Of course there are the moomlatz destinations to take into consideration,[15] but to be imperfectly honest, unlike my jaunt to Asia, I haven't looked into them this time around. I'm going into this with no preconceived ideas, expectations, goals, or rudimentary knowledge of the lower continent. Maybe because I've finally accepted that the unknown future always feels safer to me than my present reality, especially when that unknown is dangerous. Warped emotio-logic? Subconscious deathwish?

Guess we'll soon find out.

---

15 *Moomlatz* means recommended in Hebrew, and most backpacker destinations (guesthouses, restaurants, vendors) have signs that read Moomlatz to alert Israelis this is where they should eat, sleep, and not get fucked over.

PERU

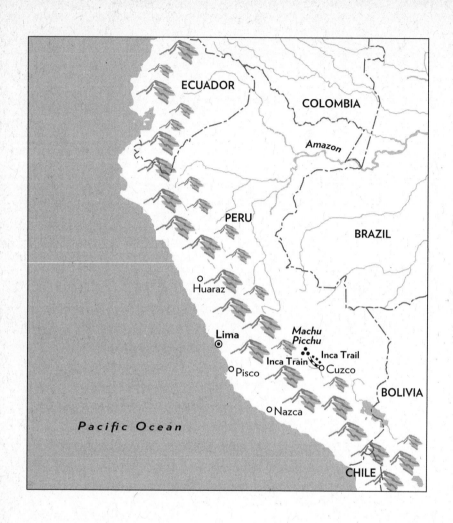

12

COULDA WALKED

I'm flying to Lima via Lacsa Airlines. All I know about Lacsa Airlines is that they're the official airline of Costa Rica and supposed to be good value for their low prices. After flying from Delhi to Bangkok on Aeroflot, an airline that believes seatbelts are a pain in the ass and a satisfying meal is an unpeeled mango served with nothing more than a napkin and good will, I am ready for anything.

I stop at Hudson News and purchase my customary pre-flight goods: two Almond Joys, one Twix, a copy of the *New Yorker*, and an intelligent book of substance that I will never read, usually revolving around Nixon or the Eisenhower administration.

Maybe I'm an idiot (don't answer that) but I've always thought non-stop and direct flights were the same thing. If you buy a direct flight from JFK to Lima, then you can expect to fly *directly* from JFK to Lima. The only reason they call it direct instead of non-stop is because it sounds less negative than non-stop, which implies that the plane's brakes don't work and a crash landing is part of the package.

But a few hours into our direct flight to Lima, we land in Honduras. I ask the flight attendant what's wrong. He looks at me as if I asked him to perform an abortion in the first-class cabin lavatory. "Nothing's wrong," he says, as several passengers push past him toward the exit and new ones board. We take off once more. Just as we reach cruising altitude, the pilot announces we're landing in Nicaragua. Now I'm really confused. I approach the flight attendant again.

"I thought this was a direct flight!"

"It *is* a direct flight."

"How can it be direct if we keep stopping?"

"It's not non-stop."

"So what the hell is 'direct'?"

"Please take your seat."

"Why?"

"People are trying to get off the plane."

I turn around. An annoyed Nicaraguan family of four point to the tarmac where their relatives are waving at me angrily.

I return to my seat and look to the other passengers for support, but they are not as perturbed as I am by this fiasco. We finally take off from the thatched hut/Nicaraguan airport with new passengers on board.

An hour later, we stop yet again, this time in San José. Before I can open my mouth the flight attendant trots over and barks, "We are a Costa Rican airline. What did you expect, that we *wouldn't* stop in San José?"

"Of course not," I reply calmly. "I wouldn't dream of questioning the fourth stop on this are-you-fucking-kidding-me direct flight. Now hand me some peanuts, please, and a blanket so I can begin my turbulation process before we land again."

"Your what?"

"Turbulation."

"What's that?"

"Not your concern. Just bring the blanket and nuts, stat!"

Turbulation!

It's easy, effective and discreet, and for women, relatively clean and neat!

❦

For those not aware, "turbulation" is my patent-pending technique that takes treatment of flying phobia to a whole new level. It's natural, simple, and is exactly how it sounds: masturbation during turbulence.

Several people have asked me, "Miss Iris, when did this wondrous technique dawn on you?" Well, I must admit, only recently, which is somewhat puzzling. God knows I've been masturbating for years now. You'd think I would've figured out that if it's fun at home it might be put to good use in other locations, especially one as stressful as a bopping aircraft. I think it occurred to me on a particularly anxiety-inducing flight when I unknowingly thrust my hand between my legs and three or four finger twitches later I spontaneously orgasmed, apologized to the mother of the ten-year-old next to me, and made it my life's mission to perfect this technique and make it crowd appropriate.

Instructions for Discreet Turbulation

Welcome to the wonderful world of turbulation! First of all, congratulate yourself on being proactive and taking action toward a better, calmer, more pleasurable flying experience, without any jail time for indecent exposure!

At this point, you must be wondering, "How on earth do I keep turbulation discreet?" Well, it's easy! The movements of the plane coupled with an isolated finger motion (see chapter four on wrist control and keeping arm movements to a minimum) will prevent anyone from realizing what's going on underneath the airline flannel blankie.

The discretionary challenge lies in the second, or "orgasm," phase of turbulation, and that involves what some cultures call "sex face" or "O-face," also known in Los Angeles as what you look like when you're lifting weights, or "ugly." While it's almost impossible to keep your face expressionless during the moment of climax, with practice you will soon be able to bite your tongue or thrust your face into the lice-ridden airline pillow upon peaking to hide any contortions in facial muscles that might occur.

13

ILLUMINATI

A word about my Uncle Shmulike. He is ten years younger than my father but looks twenty years older. He has what you might call a "colorful" past, one that was never talked about at home. It involved lots of sketchy behavior, charming outbursts, and catchy laughter. Maybe to the bank, I'm not sure. It also involved several marriages, including one to an albino lady in Provo, Utah, who kept an impressive collection of empty beer cans in the backseat of her car.

Uncle Shmulike's current squeeze is Iordana, a Peruvian twenty-something, or as my dad calls her, A lovely, simple girl from the jungles of the Amazonas."

The last time I saw Uncle Shmulike was over ten years ago on a family trip to the Sinai (back when Israel still owned it). My dad had just started dating a classy Wall Street exec named Meryl, and he was bringing her to Israel to meet me. For the occasion, he organized a "family" trip that included Uncle Shmulike and his second wife and kids. Meryl was very nice and brought me several Tiffany *don't hate me just because I've replaced your mother* bracelets, which I promptly misplaced. I was such an idiot back then. I mean, they were Tiffany bracelets, for Chrissake. Could I not have vented my rage and jealousy in a less materially damaging fashion?

Meryl actually turned out to be a lot of fun, and we all ended up having a great weekend largely because Uncle Shmulike made sure of it—buying the entire family elaborate dinners, telling me and my cousin we could get and do any-thing we wanted on the hotel premises (which translated into lots of video games and junk food), taking us all on a really expensive diving excursion. I felt bad for my dad for being upstaged by his younger brother, who always seemed to be the big man on campus when it suited him. I felt even worse for him when I found out that Uncle Shmulike was charging everything to my dad's card. Of course, my dad knew that inevitable outcome from the outset, but he was too classy to say anything, and I will always respect him for that.

♋

Lima airport smells like leather and old bananas. Uncle Shmulike defies my expectations and is on time and wait-ing for me at baggage claim, his bright white hair a familiar beacon. Iordana is standing by his side in tight jeans, spike heels, and a shirt with a thousand sequins shaped either like Michael Jackson or Jesus—I can't tell if the shape at the bot-tom is a beard or not. She is fucking gorgeous. I don't get it. How does a paunchy 50-year-old Israeli with white hair and fluctuating employment score a woman that young and hot? I mean, were *all* the males in the village already taken? Or is she just indulging some questionable middle-aged Israeli fetish?

Shmulike acts like he's overjoyed to see me. He envelops me in a bear hug, bouncing his laughter off the dirty terminal walls. Maybe he *is* overjoyed to see me. Why not give him the benefit of the doubt, I say. Iordana kisses me on both cheeks. Her hair smells like the coconut stuff Carla uses on her hair. I suddenly miss Carla very much. But not her coconut hair. That I could do without.

The three of us wait for Talia's truly non-stop flight (I'm not bitter) to arrive from Tel Aviv. In the meantime, Shmulike tells me with much drama and volume how he thought his life was over, how he thought he would never find love again, how his life was shit until he met Iordana on a Peruvian business trip, how she was just a simple girl from a tiny village in the Amazonas, but now she is his personal queen. Iordana doesn't understand a word of what he's saying and stands there silently smiling in sequined glory. Uncle Shmulike is courteous enough to translate his speech for her into impeccable Spanish. (Womanizers always seem to have a knack for foreign languages.)

My father could not be more different than his brother—a workaholic, loyal, honest, and responsible to the extreme. Nevertheless, Shmulike was their mother's favorite. No matter what my father did, how well he took care of her, how often he called her to check in, she would light up more when her sweet son Shmulike called to ask for help. Guess he made her feel needed. No wonder we all came out so damaged.

But my dad loved his brother unconditionally and never gave up on him. No matter how many times Shmulike relapsed into oblivion and then suddenly resurfaced again with a "new-start" plan, my dad always said, "This time he's changed. He's got a stable job, he's starting fresh. This time is different." So when Pop told me his brother was now married and living in domestic bliss in Lima, I didn't really believe him.

"Shmulike's working at a lighting import company!" he announced proudly.

"What the hell is a lighting import company?" I asked.

He had no idea.

જી

Talia arrives looking remarkably well rested, like one of those people who can sleep anywhere under any circumstances. Fuckerette. We hug, not quite as intensely as I would have hoped, considering we hadn't seen each other in so long. Shmulike is next. She's a bit taken aback when he thrusts her into his aftershaved armpits. She is also amazed at Iordana's hotness and ability to navigate eight-inch heels.

We head to the affluent neighborhood of Miraflores, where Shmulike has miraculously afforded himself a nice home for him and his tribal wife.

The ride allows for some probing opportunities, and I ask Shmulike what "lighting import company" means. To my amazement he describes in extensive detail the nature of the special eco-friendly streetlights he's bringing in from China that will apparently change the face of Peru. Guess dad was right!

Talia is clearly overwhelmed by Shmulike's energy and manic delivery. In her house, everyone always spoke in perfectly balanced, pleasant tones. If families were songs, hers would be by Enya; mine—Sepultura. Talia's mother specialized in hypnosis, her voice always mellifluous and somnambufabulous. (Triple word score. 176 points. Thank you.) Her dad, in contrast, was a small, adorable man who always had a light, festive energy and a smile that lit up a room. I don't know why I'm talking about these people in the past tense—they're both alive and well. Maybe it's because my memory of them is from growing up. For all I know today, they could both be raving lunatics scouring the beaches of Atlantic City for gold trinkets.

Probably not.

"How are your parents doing?" I ask her, while Shmulike speeds down the poorly lit Peruvian freeway, caressing Iordana's neck with his free hand.

"Same as usual. How about yours?"

"Yes!" Shmulike interjects, his voice careening off the four walls of the Renault. Talia cringes, unaware that humans were even capable of speaking at such volumes. "How's my brother doing?"

"Aba's doing great."

"And his wife? How's she doing?"

"Great."

"What's her name again? Marilyn?"

"Meryl."

"Right, right, Meryl. Lawyer?"

"Stocks and bonds."

"Right, right, stocks and bonds, stocks and bonds."

***

Shmulike's apartment is actually modest. Seems like he's finally calmed down and is living within his means. Dad's right again!

Talia and I take much-needed showers that involve turning on an electric water-heating device situated precariously over the showerhead. We change into our pajamas, eager for a good night's rest. Not to obsess over Talia's body since we've been through that already, but God her legs are skinny. I am not a fan of my legs. They're not fat or cankley, but they're nothing to write home about either. I used to hate my boobs too. Well, what was there to hate. They used to be very small—not mosquito-bite small, but small enough for the guys in twelfth grade to make fun of.

At the time, my mom tried to be helpful, suggesting we get me a padded bra. That sounded like a brilliant idea. We settled on a puffy B-cup with a cool clasp in the front. I couldn't wait for the next day at school when I would have breasts, everyone would be fooled, and I would be accepted into high school society in a whole new way!

The next morning I put the bra on. It felt bigger than when I had put it on in the store, and there was definitely a substantial air pocket between where my boobs ended and the padding began. I put on my favorite red shirt, watching with glee as it stretched in the chest area. I spent half an hour doing front and profile views in my bedroom mirror and headed to school a proud, busty woman.

I walked onto the schoolyard with newfound confidence, like a petite peacock with shiny new implants, reveling in everyone's stares that no doubt masked desire and envy.

I sat through first period geography class, unable to focus on the population explosion in Cairo not because my huge boobs were distracting me but because, no matter how much I tightened it, the bra strap kept falling off my shoulder. I kept fiddling with it in as inconspicuous a fashion as possible, not realizing the clasp had come undone in the process.

I walked across the courtyard to the gym. Whew. The strap seemed to have adjusted itself and was no longer a nuisance. People still stared as I walked by, but they didn't look envious. They looked . . . confused. Some even disturbed. Shit. Did I go too big? Did my boobs look ridiculous? I looked down at my chest. No, they were not too big. No, they were not ridiculous. They were just in two completely different locations—both from each other and from where boobs are normally situated. The left pad had floated up toward my shoulder, and the other had somehow made its way down to my navel. I grabbed them both before they floated out of my shirt and ran into the gym like a spineless peacock kicked in the gut by her plastic surgeon. I tore the padded monster off my body and tossed it in the trash.

I hugged my little boobies apologetically. "I will never try to augment you guys again," I whispered.

"Don't worry," they whispered back. "We will still surprise you."

And they did, somehow managing to grow to perfect proportions during the last month of my military service. They have since accumulated many fans across the globe (www.thelittleonesthatcould.com).

❧

Talia and I are already tucked in bed when Shmulike storms in.

"You ready?"

"For what?" we ask.

"We're going out!"

"*Now?*"

"Of course! The night has just started," Shmulike cries.

There's that gleam in his eye, the one that my dad had sworn had disappeared, the gleam that meant trouble. But it was gentler now, more innocent. He looks at our tired faces and opens the window to force a second wind upon us.

14

FISHY

The jazz club is a speakeasy of sorts that reeks of ceviche and corruption. There Shmulike introduces us to Chico, a tiny man straight out of a comic book, replete with square head and a tracheotomy scar.

Talia and I take our seats and soak in the fantastic music while Shmulike and Chico tell jokes and Iordana weeps in the corner. Oh shit, Iordana's weeping in the corner. I tap Shmulike on the shoulder and point to his wife who is now full on sobbing and inexplicably rubbing a piece of trout between her fingers.

"What's wrong with Iordana?" I ask.

"She cries a lot," Shmulike replies nonchalantly. "Hormones. Don't worry about it."

Iordana tosses the trout chunk onto the floor. An awkward beat. Shmulike gets back to his joke. Talia and I begin to feel uncomfortable.

"Are you okay, Iordana?" I ask quietly.

Sob, sob.

Even Chico's starting to look concerned. Shmulike gets up abruptly and points a rigid finger to the exit. Iordana obediently follows him outside. The ceviche suddenly smells like the dead fish it is. We watch as Shmulike and Iordana rail at each other in spikey Spanish, gesticulating madly. My stomach aches the way it did when my parents used to fight. I make a funny face at Talia and roll my eyes, hoping she'll think this is the first time I've witnessed such crazy behavior.

Shmulike takes Iordana in his arms and kisses her passionately. Such a skill, turning angry passion into a sexual one. Iordana is glowing, and all is now well (except for the trout I guess—he's still glued to the floor). Shmulike looks over and motions for us to come out. We obey. (What can I say? This rigid finger shit works.) Turns out the obedient little girl exists in all of us—even Chico, who leaps to attention before realizing he arrived separately and is free to stay and help the staff mop up.

We drive back to Miraflores watching Iordana and Shmulike massage each other's necks and make goo goo eyes at each other. I think our work here in Lima is done.

15

DENTAL DAM

Our first stop, as we head south towards Machu Picchu (the pinnacle of Peruvian sightseeing), is Pisco, home of the Pisco Sour cocktail and a booming cannery industry that has endowed the entire city with the smell of stinky poon. As if that wasn't enough, there is a gentle vaginal breeze that ensures we get a fresh, concentrated dose every few minutes.

No matter how many showers Talia and I take over the course of our first few hours there, we still smell like Pap smears gone awry. It's so nauseating that we can't even walk around town without falling ill. Instead, we opt to hide under the covers with deodorant sticks shoved up our noses. No wonder men always do a smell check before venturing down there.

Despite the vagininity in the air, I'm relieved to be here with Talia right now. It's definitely a fresh change of pace from Brown. Only thing that's missing are other backpackers. Men in particular. God knows I've been hungering to engage with men my own age who didn't belch beer or money into my face.

Funny, Talia's as horny as I am. I never thought of her as a highly active copulator. Although we did lose our virginity to the same pasty nebbish who had an insane collection of crisp white T-shirts. Come to think of it, Talia has had way more boyfriends than I have, the last being a short boy of Syrian descent who had an insanely thick pelt of back hair and chest hair and face hair and ear hair and nose hair. In essence, he had hair over every square inch of his entire body except his testicular region, which Talia said he trimmed diligently.

Talia figures we should head to Nazca, a much more touristy destination, where we will likely meet some actual backpackers.

Unlike Pisco, Nazca is famous for something historically substantial: the famous Nazca Lines, massive, ancient tribal figures mysteriously etched in the soil eons ago. I am actually excited to see these lines. The problem is that they can only be seen from the sky, i.e., a Cessna flight that involves vomiting one's brains out.

I tell Talia that there's no way my stomach will tolerate a tiny plane and we should consider alternatives. Talia says she is going to take the flight anyway and will just tell me about it afterward. While this makes complete sense, I feel slighted. I mean, if I can't go, then she shouldn't go either, right? Then again, why would she give up the chance to vomit and see lines at the same time? I'm just being needy and stupid.

Talia ascends to the heavens, waving at me all satisfied and sweet. I seem to have forgotten that she's always done what she wanted without thinking twice.

To be honest, I have always felt like I cared about our friendship more than Talia did. If I disappeared from her life, she wouldn't really care, but her departure from mine would devastate me. I was always the one initiating our get-togethers, and while she was always my first choice for an activity partner, I always seemed to be her second or even third. Nevertheless, our time together was always so great that I persisted with this behavior pattern, secretly hoping that she would care more and come around.

"It still stings!" I tell the Nazcan ticket seller, who nods in empathy.

"For scared children and people who vomit easily," he says, pointing to a fifty-foot ladder a few hundred feet away. I rush over and climb the ladder, camera in hand. Take that, Talia! I reach the top and look down eagerly, but all I can see is the corner of what looks like an ancient figure's big toe.

I climb back down and wait for Talia to land. I hope she's holding a barf bag. Okay, that was mean. I take it back. I hope she's holding an *empty* barf bag.

Of course, Talia skips off the plane and raves about how she didn't puke once and how awesome the figures were.

"That's fantastic!" I reply. "But did you get to see the big toe?"

"What big toe?" she asks. "There was no big toe, just a pitchfork of some kind."

"Oh, guess you missed it. That's too bad—it's the coolest part of the figure."

"Really?" she asks.

God, I'm a horrible liar. "No, I'm just kidding. I'm just frustrated I was too sensitive to get on the plane and didn't get to see anything."

"Oh. It wasn't that great."

"Really?"

"No. It was awesome."

Talia cackles like a witch; I laugh. She sketches a figure in the sand to show me what I missed. I sketch a huge toe to show her what she missed. Her sketch is a simple, elegant stick figure, mine a tattooed big toe with some sort of wart growing out of its side and little roses on the fingernail. We head back to the guesthouse, equally satisfied.

16

SOCK IT TO ME

Cuzco: the main attraction. Finally, a tangible festivity in the air, dozens of guesthouses, a quaint little square in the center of town, markets, dance clubs, and locals wearing beautifully embroidered ponchos.

Our guesthouse sits atop a steep hill. To my utter joy, dozens of Israeli backpackers (or *muchilleros* as they are known here) are milling about the lobby. They are a world apart from their Israeli counterparts who roam Asia. The muchilleros are smarter, better educated, and more interested in nature reserves and tribal customs than body massages and full-moon parties. Basically Israelis who go to Asia go to party and shtoop the locals, whereas Israelis go to South America to trek and shtoop the locals.

Their trekkie conversations are somewhat daunting. While I am a nature lover, I am an avid anti-hiker. My parents were members of the "Let's drive to the vista point and wave to nature from the car!" school versus the "Let's put on our walking shoes and windbreakers and climb up the mountain" one. It's easier to fight in a car than while hyperventilating. I don't think my dad even owns a pair of sneakers.

Talia on the other hand, delves right into the mountainous frenzy and begins to engage in animated trek talk with this girl, Pazit, a stout Israeli girl high on the tomboyometer. Pazit has harsh black bangs and numerous freckles that have grouped together in odd locations on her face, as if afraid that spreading out into sole units would lead to spontaneous combustion. She also has a deep voice, a huge gap between her two front teeth that results in a strong lisp, and a fuzzy unibrow two hairs short of the letter M. Her brown eyes bulge slightly out of their sockets in a way that makes her look really alert. Sort of like Elijah Wood. With a medium-sized log up his ass.

Pazit has been traveling through South America for over a year and has done every trek permitted by law. I immediately feel threatened by her presence. Sure, I can provide some laughs and neurosis-based anecdotes, but Pazit can offer enthusiasm for nature adventures and a fully transportable kitchen facility, which includes a special double-burner camping stove that, she makes sure to mention, is "turbo." I didn't know burners came in "turbo." I mean we're talking a burner for camping, not a fucking Corvette.

"In Huaraz, I was able to make Turkish coffee at three thousand meters above sea level!" she gloats while Talia looks on, impressed and eager. She barrages Pazit with questions about her adventures, which Pazit gladly answers, her eyebrow hairs shaking in enthusiasm. The middle ones scream, "Why are we here? We're not needed! Get us out of here, goddammit! Tweeze us, *tweeeeeze ussssss!*"

In my heightened state of neediness, I realize that every person who draws Talia away from me is terrifying. I don't like myself at all right now. I'm being ridiculous, and I know it. But as Dr. Kaufman taught me, "Be kind to yourself, and do what's good for you. And please don't finish my box of tissues each session. Thank you."

Thankfully Pazit and her threatening enthusiasm are both leaving in search of salt crystals in Bolivia, so Talia has no better option than to head downtown with me for some exploration. We trek down the hill (okay, maybe trek is a strong word, but throw me a bone here) to Cuzco's main square and head to the flea market, where dozens of toothless Inca or Aztec women (I have yet to read up on my Peruvian history, but I plan to, goddammit) are selling beautiful ponchos and socks and jewelry.

"*Que eso?*" I ask pointing to a fuzzy scarfy item in my limited Spanish.

"Alpaca." the woman replies. "Pure alpaca."

I recall alpaca being some sort of yak-like creature.

Then she points to a red poncho. "Alpaca."

"Wow. It looks totally different," I say, marveling at the wonders of weavery.

She points to an ivory-like pendant. "*Pure* alpaca."

How the fuck can all these items be made of alpaca? Do they take the baby alpacas and chop them into tiny bits so that every body part is utilized?

The woman points to a silver chain. "Alpaca." Then gold earrings. "Alpaca."

"Okay, now you're shitting me," I tell her. (Well, I actually say "*Da mi caca*," but she gets the point.)

"*No, no, alpaca! Todo alpaca!*"

The alpaca. Miracle animal. Able to produce fuzzy sweaters, gold jewelry, and ivory pendants.

Talia spots a pair of colorful socks hanging at a stall across the way.

"Sheep wool," the other woman says, beckoning us away from the alpaca Nazi.

"Aren't they cool?" Talia exclaims.

They are indeed cool.

"I *have* to have them!" Talia looks at the socks dreamily. I function as interpreter and begin the haggling process.

"*Quanto costa?*" I ask the woman.

"*Cinco dolares,*" she replies.

"Five dollars is too much," Talia says. "Tell her one dollar."

"One dollar? Isn't that pushing it a bit? These are nice socks."

"One dollar."

"Okay, *uno dollaro,*" I tell the woman, slightly embarrassed.

The woman nods her head. She's seen these kinds of Israelis before.

"*Tres dolares. No puedo un dolar!*"

"That's crazy!" Talia says, annoyed.

"Three dollars actually sounds pretty reasonable, Talia. If you want the socks just get them."

The woman's two-year-old son rears his head from some mysterious place beneath the woman's shirt.

"Forget it. Let's go," Talia says, walking away.

"*Okay, dos dolares, dos dolares!*" the woman cries. "*No puedo menos! Yo tengo bambinos!*"

Talia shakes her head and keeps walking.

"It's only two dollars, Talia. If you want the socks, you should get the socks!"

"I don't like to be ripped off. Let's forget it."

"But you want the socks?"

"Yes, I love them."

"But you're not willing to pay one extra dollar for something you really want?"

"Absolutely not. She's totally fucking me over. I will not let her win!"

"But you're the one losing out here. You're the one who wants the socks!!"

"Yeah, well, that's okay," Talia says and keeps walking. I turn back around to find the woman's two-year-old giving us the finger with one hand while wielding a large alpaca blade in the other. I fear Talia will mourn her lost sock-op for the rest of the day, but I quickly remember that Talia doesn't really mourn anything.

Four stalls later Talia finds an identical pair of socks. She gets them for one dollar.

"Told you!" she says, a triumphantly tranquil smile on her face.

17

IT BEGAN IN AFRIKAAAA

In preparation for our jaunt this evening to the moom-latz dance club, Mama Africa, Talia and I don our most asset-accentuating outfits; I wear my "Damn, her ass looks good!" tight jeans and my roomy "Can't quite tell how big her boobs are" T-shirt, while Talia wears her roomy "She might have an ass—it's hard to say" jeans and a "Holy shit, look at those jugs!" tight T-shirt.

Most men probably wish they could cut and paste us together, but lucky for us we're in South America and the pickins are slim. It's nice to be big fish in a small pond— why choose otherwise? I can't imagine working at a mod-eling agency or hanging out in Sweden or Ukraine—the damage to one's self-esteem would be devastating. Even brief visits to these locales border on masochism.

Mama Africa is a cramped underground cave with wood-paneled walls, a low ceiling, lots of sweaty backpack-ers, and '80s music. Talia and I stroll in. All eyes turn to us.

Actually to Talia's breasts, which of course have the advantage over my ass, which happens to be behind my body. I should have walked in backward. Note to self for next time.

The high-school dance standards pound away: "Superstition," "Respect," "In the Name of Love." Within seconds, Talia's dancing with a narrow Israeli dude of Yemenite descent. He has a cute face but squiggly chemically assisted blonde hair. I am left dancing with myself, feeling stupid. Oh God, "Bohemian Rhapsody" just started. Kill me now. Perfect time to pee.

Someone has been in the bathroom forever. Going in now is almost as scary as when people leave the toilet lid down. Lifting it up without knowing what's lurking inside the bowl is as terrifying as unprotected sex in Rio. Finally the culprit emerges. Holy Christ. He's a local. The most gorgeous local I've ever seen. The guy Mel Gibson would cast if he were making *Apocalypto: A Love Story.* It's as if Johnny Depp, Clive Owen, and an Inca sperm donor had a child together: luscious olive skin, broad shoulders, long shiny black hair, big brown eyes, a perfect Roman nose, and remarkably appealing teeth.

He eyes me for a beat.

Goddammit woman, why didn't you wait with your ass facing the door? Don't you learn?

"*Que linda,*" he says, admiring my face. I forgot about my face. It's not so bad apparently.

His name is Raoul, and he is a Cuzconian. Cuzcino. Cuzack. Whatever. He's *hot*—and he is clearly smitten with me. Thank the lord for small ponds.

We dance for a while. At some point Talia heads back to the guesthouse with Ahmed blondie to get her Yemenite on. Raoul and I take a seat on a pile of fleece jackets in the corner. Not many words are exchanged, not because we are too busy making out, but because Raoul speaks no English, and words like "how much" and the number five don't leave much room for meaningful conversation. I can't tell if Raoul is smart or dumb as a doorknob; when you're that handsome, the world assumes you're not bright (God giveth, God taketh away), but that's not really fair, is it? And does it really matter? It's not like Raoul is coming back to live with me at the Grad Center to discuss postmodernist tropes over some Celestial Seasonings. But I can't help it. I need to see what's beyond the beauty. *I'm that deep.*

Actually, scratch that. Right now all I want to experience is the magic that is naked Inca. I can see it now: my grandchildren sitting at my feet, staring up at Grandma for words of wisdom. "Yes, my beloved little ones," I would tell them, "Lust can conquer all. You may be short and neurotic and not have boobs as big as your best friend, but, when everyone else looks kinda mediocre, the hottest guy in town will want to fuck you, and you need to know that and enjoy that and not give a shit if he has a brain. Now be a doll and get your grandmother her bedpan."

I can only imagine what Raoul's life is like, fucking different backpackerettes every night, not bothering to learn another language, thereby saving his small brain from actually having to respond to women's unnecessary requirements for dialogue. The man has it *down.*

Raoul takes me outside and kisses me. I try to erase the mental image of thousands of mouths before me and enjoy the moment.

"Do you want to go back to your place?" I ask. (In essence, it comes out as "From one to five, how much you want me and your house?")

"Sure," he says, "but my friend is staying there."

"Your friend?"

"Yes, Lital. She is beautiful Israeli girl."

What the fuck?

"Don't worry, she is like sister. She stay with me, but she happy if you come stay too."

I guess that makes sense. Don't get all high maintenance now, woman. None of the other backpackerettes did.

"Sure, I'd love to meet Lital."

Raoul and I rush back to his place, equally horny and excited.

His ground-floor pad is nestled in between two *Best Pizza in Cuzco!* joints. He opens the door to reveal a room inhabited entirely by a large bed. In the bed lies a tiny pixie-ish blonde woman, who looks like Tweety Bird pushing forty. She puts down the book she's reading.

"Raouli!" she yelps, jumping out of the bed in sensible off-white underwear. Her face may be 40 but her body is 14-year-old boy.

She gives Raoul a kiss on the cheek and then looks at me.

"*Ahalan*, I'm Lital," she says, hugging me on her tippy toes.

Raoul strips down to his A.C. Milano boxer briefs and hops into bed. Lital hops back into bed too. I must say I didn't anticipate one sleeping site for the three of us. How are Raoul and I supposed to have crazy Inca sex with this Tolkienesque creature literally lying right there for the duration?

"You coming to bed?" Raoul asks, making room for me between the two of them.

My options are pretty limited. Leave now or dive in . . .

FROM THE PRODUCERS WHO BROUGHT YOU
The Little Mermaid AND *Finding Nemo*
COMES THE NEW PIXAR PORN EXTRAVAGANZA:
*Tweety Pan and Raoul Cuzack Double-Team
The Princess of Zion!*
Now available on Blu-Ray

I strip down to my thong and tank top and crawl into the bed, nestling awkwardly between the two of them. The bed definitely looked wider from a foot away. In fact, my left leg is touching Raoul's and my right Lital's. Bitch got toenails.

Raoul starts kissing me. Now, if Tweety Pan were actually watching or even snoozing innocently beside us, I might have felt some semblance of a kinky sexual vibe, but she just goes back to reading her book, flipping the pages faster and louder than normal reading would warrant.

Raoul pulls me closer, the page-turning more a crumpling action now. This is getting ridiculous. I don't know how the other backpackerettes did it, but I cannot.

"Let's save this for another night, Raoul."

"*Bien, Irisita, no problemo. Buenas noches.*" He turns off the light, and moves onto his stomach, preventing any spoonage opportunity.

I move closer to him, trying to avoid leg contact with Tweety Pan, but she keeps moving her legs closer to mine. I finally give up, letting her big toenail dig into my calf muscle. I'm too exhausted to fight.

I fall asleep fairly quickly but awaken a few hours later with a horrible feeling that something bad has just happened. I open my eyes. The windowless room is pitch black. What's wrong? I mean, besides the fact that I'm sharing a bed with an Incan manwhore and a prepubescent yet aging cartoon character.

Raoul and Tweety are sleeping like twin babies, their shallow breathing in perfect sync. I take a breath and realize with dread what has happened. I reach down to feel my underwear. Yep, it's damp. Über damp. I've gotten my period. We're talking heavy flow. Fuck. Did I leak on his sheets? I must have leaked on his sheets. I'm wearing thong underwear, for Chrissake. Only this could happen to me, only *I* could get my period while nestled in a foreign bed flanked by strangers.

I turn on the light, and lo and behold there is a massive bloodstain on the sheets, right where it should be. In a panic, I take off my drenched underwear and throw on my jeans, stuffing them with so much toilet paper that I am left with a penis-like bulge in my crotch.

"*Todo bien, Irisita?*" Raoul asks fuzzily.

Shit. I quickly toss my bloody underwear under the bed. "Yes, of course, of course. Just taking a break from spooning. Intimacy issues, you know how it is . . . "

Before he questions any further, I hit the light switch and rush out, praying to the Saint of Embarrassing Menstrual Events that Raoul never checks under his bed and prefers to change his sheets with his eyes closed.

ↂ

So much for my first sexcapade in South America. Back at the guesthouse, Talia is showered and ready for breakfast. She has a Yemenite post-coital glow about her and looks confused as I enter all crusty and frustrated.

"How was last night?" she asks.

"Fine. I got my period all over Raoul's bed, which he shares with a middle-aged eagle woman."

"Oh no!"

"Yeah, I ran out before they woke up. I did leave my bloody underwear as a memento, though."

"That's fucked up."

FLASHBACK: LEWD INTERLUDE #1, OR PREVIOUS PERIOD TRAUMA 3B

A week after my return from Asia, I headed down to the Sinai Desert to soften the transition back to normal living. I was accompanied by Rami, a young gentleman blessed with black curls, a potbelly, and unclear intentions.

It was summertime, and the Sinai was unbearably hot. We were staying in a wood hexagon-shaped hut that had huge cut-out square holes as windows. We shared it with a few other stoners who came to Sinai to smoke, snorkel, and recoup. We'd all been lying on the sand all day, and I was trying to find an opportune moment to go back to the hut and change my tampon when nobody else was there, since the actual bathroom doubled as a fat fly sauna and getting there involved a Sisyphean climb up a massive, scorching hot sand dune and ogling Bedouins.

To my delight, our hut was empty. Mind you, I could have been honest with Rami, but we were at that fresh phase in the relationship where I was still leading him to believe I didn't shit, fart, or bleed out of my hoo-ha, so no mention of my cycle had come up.

I tried to find an angle where nobody could see me through the massive square window holes. I removed the used tampon and had the other one ready when suddenly I spotted Rami heading back to the hut at breakneck speed. Why? What did he want? And what was I going to do with the bloody tampon in my hand?

The window opposite the entryway was my only option. I'd toss it through there and then pick it up out of the sand the minute Rami left. Perfect.

I flung the tampon, discus-like, toward the window. It was supersize and displayed an impressive trajectory. My aim, however, was not impressive, and the objet d'art missed the window by a foot and smacked into the wall with a wet thud, sticking to the wood as if my blood were Superglue. I watched, horrified, as it stuck there for a moment before slowly oozing down the wall, leaving a long bloody trail in its wake, finally landing on top of my sleeping bag with a wet *plmpf.*

Rami entered to find me in my underwear looking like a menstruating deer in headlights. I prayed that he wouldn't notice the blood on the wall.

"Oh my God, is that *blood* on the wall?" he asked, appalled.

"Uh, yeah . . . huge mosquito. Just killed it. HUGE. Must have been pregnant. I feel horrible, like a real killer."

The tampon looked up at me from its resting place. I could hear it hiss through its drenched fibers. "You're a fucking coward, lady. I'm a necessary part of the female cycle. You bleed on me and discard me and can't even acknowledge your cruelty with dignity. I hate you."

Rami looked at the blood path like a frustrated art director. He shook his head, grabbed a book from his bag, and ambled back to the beach.

I grabbed the pissed-off tampon, wrapped it in toilet paper, and headed deep into the desert for a dignified cremation ceremony, away from judgmental spectators, family, and friends.

It was the least I could do.

18

FICO DE GALLO

As all previous Israelis before us, Talia and I have two moomlatz goals in Cuzco: seeing Machu Picchu and going white-water rafting. And so we hop down the hill towards the moomlatz Rafting Company office, which is filled with notes in Hebrew raving about the staff and photos of satisfied Israelis around toasty campfires. "Three rafts per group," the flat-faced office manager says, "one guide per raft. The group leaving today is full. You can leave on the next one in three days, but you need to choose which guide you want now."

The first guide is an opiated old fart named Fico, the second a tiny Peruvian named Marco, and the third a sexy Chilean named Gustavo. They all happen to be right outside the office loading gear into the van for the group that leaves in an hour. Fico looks our way, his eyes exuding an age-old wisdom despite their stoned glassiness.

"We should go with Fico," Talia says. "He's had the most experience."

"But he's so opiumed out he probably can't remember his experience," I counter. "What about the hot guy? Nothing like a sexy Chilean folding a life jacket into a tiny square to get the juices flowing."

We debate for a bit. Age ends up winning over beauty. We're women, we know what's important. (And I will just make my move on Gustavo at the campsite.)

The guides have finished packing up the van and are about to leave with group one. Two Israeli girls of equal plumpage ask me to take a photo of them before their departure. They are from Holon, a pseudo shithole near Tel Aviv, and are super sweet and excited. They saved for this trip for a year, and it's a dream come true for them. Their enthusiasm is contagious and reminds me that I'm as lucky as they are to be here.

Gustavo puts his hand on their backs. "*Vamonos!*" he orders sexily, nudging them toward the van with a Colgate smile.

"Have a great time! See you in three days!" we call out as they drive off.

⁊

Three days later, we show up at the rafting office just as group one is returning. The two Israeli girls are sitting in the same seats as when they left. Funny how that always happens—nobody tells you to sit in the same seat, but you always do. I wave at them excitedly.

They don't wave back. They look miserable. Devastated, in fact.

The van door whooshes open. Fico jumps out and rushes into the office, whispering something to the manager. Marco is wiping tears from his face. And Gustavo . . . well, Gustavo does not come out of the van.

"Where's Gustavo?" I ask.

The girls burst out crying. "He died."

"What? What do you mean he died? How?"

They spit out the story in between sobs and coughs. "Our raft . . . flipped over and . . . he got caught . . . under a rock and . . . they couldn't get him out . . . and he . . . died . . . he died."

Fico emerges from the office with a fresh look of focus and determination. "Okay, group one, everybody into the van. We're running late!"

The other Israelis in our group start piling in, Talia included.

"Where are you going?" I ask.

"What do you mean? We're going rafting."

"The guide just *died!* How could we go rafting now?"

"Accidents happen," Fico chimes in soothingly, like Morgan Freeman's older, baked Latin cousin.

I grab Talia by the shoulders. "The Guide. Was Killed," I repeat. "The *GUIDE* was KILLED! What kind of chance do we have?"

"They won't give us a refund," Talia says, matter of fact.

"That's why you want to go? Because they won't give us a refund?!"

"I'm just saying. We paid for it; we should go."

"I don't believe this."

Fico puts his hand on my back. Memories of Gustavo and all that could have been flood through my veins.

"You have nothing to worry about," Fico velvets. "You come with me, you'll be fine. Gustavo was reckless. I read the river like a book. He raced through it like a tabloid magazine."

Maybe I *am* overreacting; we are in good hands. Accidents happen! It's obvious I'm just channeling my mother. She was always so terrified something would happen to me that she instilled the same anxiety in me. It's her fault I'm so fucking neurotic, right, Dr. Kaufman? You know what? I will fight that part of me. I will fight it, and I will be adventurous and risk my life on this white-water rafting trip just so Talia feels like she got her money's worth and I don't feel like a pussy.

Let's do this!

19

HARD!!!

We arrive at base camp in the early afternoon. Fico helps Talia buckle her life jacket, which is clearly not designed for larger cup sizes. Mine on the other hand closes instantly. The clasps laugh as I bring them together from either side. "Can you believe how effortless this is?" they squeal. "Even that Somalian boy from last week wasn't this easy! Hahahahahhahaaaaaa!"

Once we are all jacketed, Fico and Marco bring us to the riverbank. I'm assuming they want to calm our nerves, which are still pretty fucking shaky.

"Hello, everyone," Fico says, his calm voice somehow booming over the roaring rapids down the way. "We will be rafting for three days. Once we start, there is no turning back. You break a leg, you will have to live with it broken and untended for three days, so safety is of *utmost* importance. You listen to what I tell you in the water, and you do it. IMMEDIATELY. I have three commands: 'Forward,' you row forward *hard*. 'Stop,' you stop *hard*. And 'back,' you row backward *hard*. If you do not, we are in danger of flipping over, is that clear?"

What's clear, Ficoman, is that this shit is dangerous, and we're fucking crazy for doing it. Maybe it's some sort of covert extermination technique orchestrated by some satellite office of Hamas or an Iranian fan of the outdoors. "Forget suicide bombings, let's just send them on a level-6 rafting trip with no helmets. Brilliant! Don't worry about the Chilean. He was expendable."

Fico goes quiet, suddenly sullen. "I'm honored to announce that we also have a job to do," he says, with tragic military flair. "As you may know, on our last run, Gustavo, our beloved third guide, was killed. We put his body in a sleeping bag and kept him in the cold water to keep it fresh." Fresh dead body. Nice. "But on our final night, the sleeping bag disengaged from the rock we tied it to and disappeared. The family is very distraught, and so it is our job to find the body."

"It is?" I blurt, confused as to how we became Chilean body patrol. I lean over to Talia. "Is this what you call getting your money's worth?"

She shrugs.

The way I see it, there's life-endangering thrill, and then there's stupidity. There's paying money for the life-endangering thrill, and then there's searching for your guide's body while on this life-endangering thrill—and that's in a whole other category of stupidity.

ℰℐ

Once in the water, Fico's safety briefing proves worthless. I can't hear a bloody word he barks at us over the roar of the water thwacking into my head. *Forward! Stop!* and *Back!* all sound like BAH! BAH! BAH!

Nevertheless, we manage to get a good groove going, and I begin to enjoy myself. I get the appeal now: the rush of the rapids, the mastery of the terrain. Fico indeed reads the river like a book, and it's enthralling to behold.

Up ahead is a sharp turn and what looks like a particularly hairy stretch. Fico's face goes sinister. This is where Gustavo met his maker. My heart starts pounding a mile a minute. Talia's life vest bursts open in panic.

"BAH BAH!" Fico yells. We all start rowing in different directions. Come on Fico, get a fucking megaphone. "BAH BAH BAH!" he yells even more frantically, realizing the raft is not going the way he intended. He's staring at me directly now, screaming "BAH BAH BAH!!!" I can't row in any direction, the water is getting too crazy. The raft is bending and bouncing like a ping pong ball. "BAH BAH BAH!" He screams in my face. What the *FUCK*, Fico? Stop looking at me! Nobody is doing it right, why are you picking on me?

Fico suddenly grabs my head and shoves it into the base of the raft a *nanosecond* before a protruding boulder would have sliced it right off.

Fuck. Fuck fuck fuckity fuck. My heart pounds my eardrums with double mallets. They thwack rhythmically for an entire hour, then to my surprise, gradually take on a different rhythm, less death march, more Tito Puente.

By day two, I've become an expert at deciphering Fico's grunts, and I row *hard*. We unfortunately haven't found the Chilean Popsicle yet, since that would have been the perfect ending to my Latin outdoor adventure saga. Think about it—my own Jewish version of *Alive*! And let's be honest, I'm more bad-ass than any of those whiney rugby players. (I can tell you for a fact that if our *arroz con pollo* started running low I would eat my fellow raft buddies in a heartbeat.)

By the time we reach the end stretch, I don't want to leave. I'd raft all the way to Alaska right now if someone showed me the way and provided some healthy snacks. There's something to be said for diving willingly into a paid suicide mission, braving raging currents, having your cheek slammed into weathered rubber, and watching grown men pretend to struggle with a life-jacket clasp for forty-five minutes straight. This is the stuff that builds true character, that makes you appreciate life's fragility, that sends your fight-or-flight instinct into complete disarray, that transports you to an altered state where concern over survival pushes out all petty neuroses, leaving no room for feeling lonely or depressed or victimized or even happy or normal or content—just alive.

20

REALLY?

We return to Cuzco empty-bodied. Gustavo's family is so disappointed that I wonder whether his actual death was the second most painful thing about his death. I ask Talia when she wants to leave for Machu Picchu.

"There's a group that leaves for the Inca Trail tomorrow," she says.

When did she have time to find out that information without me? I too have some information. "There's a train that can take us there in three hours."

"Pazit said the trail is amazing." Pazit. I should have killed her when I had the chance.

"Yeah but the train is quicker so we can spend more time at the actual site . . . "

"I'll just meet you back here in five days," Talia declares.

"What?" I ask, shattered. "Don't you want me to come with you?"

"You don't like hiking."

"Well, why would I? I mean, sure, it's exhilarating—at first. The crisp air, the sound of crunching branches or streams or whatever nature-item happens to be under your feet, but after half a mile or so it just seems silly. I mean, get me to the vista point already. Hiking three days to get to Machu Picchu is like listening to an entire album on cassette tape. We have CDs now. Let's skip a track!"

Apparently I lost Talia at "silly."

"What's the problem, Iris? You don't like hiking, and I do."

"Yeah, but you didn't even invite me, you just decided to go. You can still invite me even if you know I don't want to come."

Talia doesn't see the logic in this. Maybe because it's not logical, but isn't that what friends do for each other? Make them feel wanted? Make sacrifices? It's clear she doesn't want me. And if that's the case, why the hell are we traveling together?

"Doesn't matter, that's fine." I say, atypically passive aggressive. "I'll just meet you back here in five days like you said."

"Great!"

Talia smiles like a true winner. I think she's always felt like a winner, not in an arrogant way, but in a way only non-neurotic people from very well balanced households can feel—no guilt, no worrying about hurting other people's feelings, just doing what they want, what makes sense, and keeping healthy boundaries. Sounds like heaven. Actually, heaven is probably more accessible to me than Talia's way of life.

I pout—a pout so substantial Gustavo can spot it from his watery grave. But Talia doesn't seem to notice, and I follow her back to our guesthouse, frustrated by my own frustration.

I guess I'm afraid that breaking up our duo unit for even a few days will destroy it completely. Then again, if it's strong enough, that won't happen, right? But I can't deny the fear in me, that horrible fear of abandonment that permeates every moment of my being. Do other people feel like this? Maybe it's normal. Maybe I've just spent so many years alone or afraid of getting close to others that I feel weird when I actually get a perfectly normal urge for companionship, a healthy desire to not be alone. How ironic for someone who has such an extreme fear of solitude, I end up spending more time alone than anyone I know.

21

KOO KOO ROO

I envision the Inca Train to be a quaint red caboose with gold INCA TRAIN lettering on the side. I don't know why I have this picturesque image in my head. After all, I've been to Third World countries before and ridden their shitty trains, and they *always* smell like ass and are filled with livestock and horny men attempting to first find my breasts and then grab them. Why am I then surprised to discover that in reality the Inca Train is a three-car dump truck filled with horny locals, livestock, and ass smell?

Sadly, there are no empty seats left, just the grimy aisle. I find a crate of yucca in close proximity to an ugly stray chicken that has either voluntarily fled his cage or was shunned by his sexier chicken brothers. It's only a fifty-mile ride, I tell myself, shielding my leg from the chicken that is now nibbling on my shin, a hearty hunger in his chickeny eyes.

To my delight, I realize that there are two muchilleros already plopped down in the aisle near me, smoking a big fat joint. One is Ziv—a tall, doughy, dim man with a sizable gap between his front teeth, and the most turquoise eyes I have ever seen and almost no pupils to speak of. A fat joint sits between his lips, and I find myself getting high from just breathing his exhalations. His partner in crime, Yoram, another pothead, happens to be the son of the Israeli Head of Intelligence. He is super skinny and has an evil face. He's not as happy as Ziv but compensates with a sharp wit.

The train chugs slowly down the tracks, so slowly that, if John Goodman were sprawled across them, we could run him over, and he would still survive. (I choose John Goodman for the sake of realism. A frailer member of the species, like Cher for example, would at least suffer some rib damage or a hairline fracture in her wrist.) Ziv and Yoram fall asleep instantly, bodies erect, necks limp. I assume we'll pick up speed once we get some momentum going, but neither seems to be happening.

The train suddenly comes to a complete stop. There's no way we've arrived already. Maybe another train needs to pass. Our train kicks into reverse and starts inching its way back to Cuzco. Shit. Is something wrong? Nobody looks alarmed or even surprised. The train keeps heading in reverse.

I nudge Ziv awake. He looks at me, confused. Jesus Christ, his eyes are astounding. How on earth does he keep his pupils so small like that all the time?

"What's up? Are we going backward?" he asks, the tooth gap allowing a bit of brain to traverse it.

"I think we're heading back to Cuzco," I say.

"Oh," he replies, oblivious to the ramifications that this new development has on our plans to see Machu Picchu that afternoon.

Yoram's still asleep. His eyebrows are arched so high that it looks like Satan is holding a pitchfork under the middle of them. God, he looks mean. Mean and pervy.

MOISHE THE RIPPER
Directed by Tim Burton
Starring
Yoram Cohen as Moishe
Helena Bonham Carter as Rivka
and Johnny Depp as the Goy Detective
Coming soon to a theatre near you!

* This film has not yet been rated.

The train stops again. We wait at a complete standstill for half an hour. Ziv and I smoke a joint. The locals don't seem to mind. (They realize chicken ass always smells more festive when marijuana is added into the mix.) The train moves forward for a few feet, then back for a few feet more. This cycle continues several times.

I ask the chicken owner what the hell is going on. He tells me that it's an engineering necessity—the train has to go backward before it can move forward.

Sounds like my life.

22

MACHU SHITTY

A word of advice: When visiting any sort of ancient ruin, always opt for a guide, even if it's some local shlub with a pamphlet and broken English who smells like sweat and incompetence. Because without one you might as well not bother visiting the ruin at all. Take it from me, as I am currently standing alongside Yoram and Ziv in front of Macchu Picchu, an official wonder of the world, as we try to marvel at . . . a pile of rubble.

And we do try. We run through the usual "Ooh, how'd they get all those rocks uphill, those ancient simple non-muscular peoples?" And the popular "Ooh, how'd they build those large, boring, kind-of-complicated triangular structures with those big rocks without any real tools or fancy equipment?" But without a guide we are left clueless and bored.

Not that the guide's answers would have been more satisfying. "See those four rocks with the grass growing in the middle of them? That used to be the Inca leader's main banquet hall," he would say, at which point he'd smoke a cigarette and sweat some more, while you stood there imagining some sort of lavish Inca bar mitzvah of sorts with thumping tribal music and animalistic sex before remembering it was just four rocks you were staring at and that was a feeling of idiocy, not awe, that was overpowering you.

We decide then that the only thing to do at this point is climb the daunting mountain that overlooks the entire site and smoke a bowl. The climb is arduous but worth it, the view undeniably astounding. The Machu rubble, more obscure from a distance, seems somehow more complete. With all the little tourists and their guides milling about . . . from up here it actually looks like the Torah fest is in full swing!

I have to say I feel pretty cool right now, staring down at the multitudes, and so I do what I always do when I feel cool: I take off my shirt and show my boobs. The tourists below wave in gratitude at my visual gift that, compared to Machu Shitty, requires less imagination to actually enjoy.

23

HUGGIE BEAR

Talia returns from her Inca Trail as effervescent as a Pellegrino-doused Alka Seltzer. I make a point of giving her a boundary-filled hug, but can't control the slight neediness that peeks through in the pressure level upon release. You know, that extra little squeeze that screams "WHY'D YOU LEAVE ME? I'M JUST A LITTLE KID! I MISSED YOU SO MUCH OH MY GOD I'M SO HAPPY YOU'RE BACK PLEASE DON'T DO THAT AGAIN. YOU KNOW, LEAVE ME."

Talia pats me on the back lightly. In hug world, of course, the pat is death. It says, "I'm hugging you out of obligation," or in opposite-sex world, "I'm not attracted to you. Let's just be friends, and even that idea makes me a little queasy. In fact, I'd rather you never call me again unless you have a hot friend I could meet and cause subsequent drama and hurt feelings with."

Talia's back-pat immediately shifts the balance of power in her favor, and before I can joke about the Inca Train she

Comprehensive Hug Guide
(Including hand-endings)

1. Codependent hug (see above)
2. Lust hug with slow release (limited to married, horny, or in the middle of a break-up people hugging single desirable parties)
3. One-sided let's just be friends hug, with or without pat (unbalanced pressure optional)
4. Bro hug
5. Girl to girl hug
6. Girl to girl hate hug with cheek graze
7. WASP hug with flattened hand
8. Are your boobs real? hug
9. Do you have boobs? hug
10. Feel my boner hug
11. Crushing family member hug
12. Unconditional hug (extremely rare, possibly non-existent)

launches into a gushing Niagraic flow about how the trail was amazing. She goes into great detail about the people in her group, the astounding vista points in the mountains, and, just as I feared, the unbelievably effective and informative guide who took them through Machu Picchu. I feel as if a knife had been thrust into the little Inca experience corner of my heart.

I want to tell her that I think what she did was lame and that I resent her for not fulfilling my needs, which consist mainly of making me feel better, less alone, loved and understood. But I don't say a thing. Maybe I believe that if it doesn't come from Talia naturally and unprompted then I don't want it anyway, or maybe I fear that asking for something and not getting it will hurt a lot more than just wallowing in the pain of its absence.

The reality is Talia and I seem to be traveling like two business partners, going from one little adventure to the next, sometimes together, sometimes apart, sometimes fun, sometimes not. It all feels so meaningless.

Well, except the boob display I gave on the top of the big mountain. That was meaningful.

"Wait—*you* climbed up the big mountain?" Talia asks, a pang of jealousy and shock in her voice.

"Yeah, you guys didn't?" I ask, smelling almond-scented opportunity.

"No, we only got there at sunset and weren't allowed to climb after dark. How was it?"

A strong sense of victory bubbles up inside of me, not in a *Holy shit, I won the race* kind of way, but in a *Holy fucking shit, I finally won the race* kind of way. Not that we were competing, but it still feels good to come out on top for once.

I describe the view in detail, focusing on the wind blowing against my supple breasts and Ziv and Yoram's looks of awe at the sights before them. Talia laughs.

"I missed you," she suddenly says, her internal wall reduced from cement security to wire mesh, albeit for a brief moment.

I pat her lightly on the shoulder. "I missed you too."

For the first time in our friendship, it dawns on me that Talia also has issues. Sure, in terms of the emotional-mess spectrum, I'm black beans and mashed potatoes all over the floor, and she's just a water spill, but still! Something is clogged in both of us, and maybe it's my job to help heal her too. Maybe I will heal me through healing her. That's kind of annoying—now my healing is dependent on her healing and she's not nearly neurotic enough to care about changing, so I'm pretty much screwed.

"Where to next?" I ask, eager to continue.

"Pazit went trekking through the snowcapped mountains of Huaraz and says we *have* to go."

My stomach tightens. I breathe deep and embark on my first attempt at healthy adult communication. *Just remember—don't whine like a child.*

"I don't wanna go to Huaraz!!" I whine childishly. But I stop, take another deep breath, and manage a more Kathleen Turneresque delivery. You can do this. "I know you like hiking, and I don't, but we *are* traveling together, and we have to compromise sometimes, Talia. I'd rather we head into Ecuador. *Together.*"

Talia's expression doesn't change.

"Okay," she says, turning around to pack her bag.

Wow. This shit actually works. I can't believe it! Be prepared world. I'm growing, I can feeeel it.

24

SHINING PATH PORTA-POTTY

We arrive at the bus station in Cuzco, only to be informed that several buses en route to the Ecuadorian border have been hijacked by Shining Path guerrillas—and by "hijacked" they mean backpackers were taken hostage, looted, pillaged, and raped.

As much as the idea of a guerrilla shining his path down my poonani sounds kinky and exciting, Talia and I board another bus that will take ten extra hours but avoids the danger zone.

Three hours in, I feel a very strong urge to urinate. Considering we have a bazillion-hour drive ahead of us, I push past the unwashed masses slumped in the aisle and ask the driver to stop.

"No," he says, not even turning my way (which is fine by me, considering he's driving erratically as it is).

"I have to pee, *señor.*"

"No stop till border."

"How far is the border?"

"Who knows, it varies."

Great.

"Sir, could you please stop for just a moment?"

"No."

He swerves the bus a bit, throwing me and my combustible bladder off balance. I inch my way back to my seat in increased urinary discomfort.

"You don't look so good," Talia says, concerned.

"I really need to pee, and the asshole driver won't stop."

I take my seat, cringing.

"Why don't you pee in a bag?"

"What?"

"I'll give you a plastic bag, and you can just pee into that."

It sounds crazy, but at this point I see no other option. Talia takes a bag of tangerines she has stashed in her backpack, unloads the fruit, and hands it to me. I look around. The other passengers don't seem to notice. How the hell am I going to manage this? With awkward effort, I stick the plastic bag into my jeans and try to position it over my pee hole. It's harder than it sounds.

"Wait!" Talia cries. "Check for holes first!"

"What?"

"Check if the bag has any holes first!"

Good point. I take the bag out of my pants, and there is a dime-sized hole that would have led to complete golden showering all over my legs and jeans.

"Fuck. Do you have any other bags?"

"Nope. That was it."

Pee pain has now spread to my entire abdominal cavity, and every bump on the road feels like an internal earthquake. With tears in my eyes, I limp toward the driver for a second attempt. "*Señor*. Ruler and master of the bus world. *Por favor*. I'm begging you. I need to pee. Please stop the bus for just a minute."

He turns to find me weeping, one hand cradling my stomach, the other between my legs to plug the pending flow.

"No."

I wipe the tear away and return to my seat, thinking of dry things like prunes and old people.

The bus comes to a screeching halt.

"That annoying girl that has to pee?" the driver calls out.

"Yes?" I call back.

"Go do it. *Now!*"

I grab my roll of toilet paper and charge through the crowd like a linebacker. The midday sun is oppressive but welcoming. I limp away from the bus looking for a tree or shrub to hide behind but there's nothing but flatlands for miles. Crap. Getting out of view is impossible. It doesn't help that the passengers are all glued to the windows, eager to watch the spectacle.

Fuck it.

I crouch down in full view of everyone and begin to pee. And pee. And pee. The spectators watch as a new yellow creek forms before their eyes. On and on it goes, swirling and winding and swirling and winding, with no end in sight. Where did I store all this liquid?

The driver kicks the bus into gear. Shit, he's about to leave me here. Talia motions to hurry up. I push the last spurt out and wipe quickly.

But wait. I can't leave a mound of toilet paper in the pure Peruvian desert like this. I must burn it, as all eco-conscious urinators do. Talia shakes her head. I struggle with the lighter. The driver starts to pull away. I race back to the bus, leaving a burning mound of TP in my wake.

I re-board, relieved but guilt-ridden.

"Sorry about the littering," I announce. (Or, "I give garbage" as proper translation would have it.)

"Yes, you do," the driver says, cracking a smile.

ECUADOR

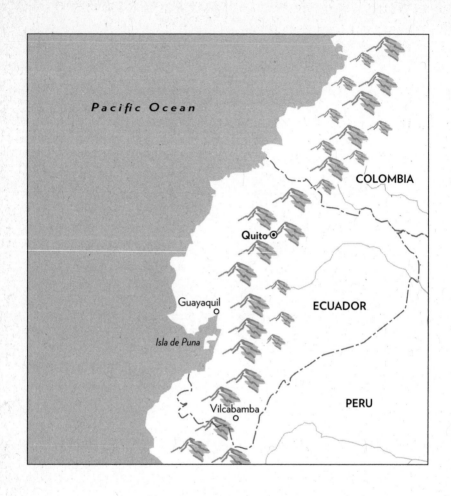

25

ANIMAL CRACKERS

We arrive at Guayaquil at dawn. Despite the low light of sunrise, it is immediately clear that the only reason to stay in this town is to go to the Galapagos Islands. The locals are also aware of this fact, judging from the hundreds of *Galapagos!* posters on every storefront.

Two questions. First, can we afford to spend an exorbitant amount of money to see this world-famous attraction? Second, do we really want to see animals weird enough to be siphoned off to their own island? More to the point, do we really want to immerse ourselves in a leper colony of freaky creatures that are told they are unique just to feel better about their evolutionary downfall?

No. Absolutely not.

"Let's get out of here," Talia says.

"Wait, I almost forgot! Carlos lives in Guayaquil! He owns a shrimp and banana farm. We could surprise him!"

"Is Carlos the guy with the testicle jeans?"

"That's the one."

"Cool!"

We rush over to a pay phone.

Ring, ring.

"*Si?*"

Carlos's voice is considerably higher than I remember. I really have to talk to him about his choice of below-the-waist apparel.

"Hey Carlos! It's me, Iris!"

Carlos takes a moment. "Iris," he says, as if announcing a score at the Olympic gymnastics finals.

"I'm here! In Guayaquil! With my friend Talia! Can you believe it? I'm actually in Guayaquil!" Ooh, I hope he doesn't take that to mean "Can you believe I'm actually here in this pointless shithole thank God you have that Darwin-fest to keep your city's economy alive."

"Carlos is not here at the moment," he says, attempting to speak in a much lower vocal register.

I was not expecting this charade.

"Carlos, come on. I know it's you. Why are you pretending to sound like a man?" Now I know *that* sounded shitty. Too late to backpedal since Carlos has already launched into what sounds like a pre-prepared speech.

"Carlos is not here at the moment. But he asked me to tell you that he has not forgiven you and does not want to see you ever again. And you really should not be speaking his name in public."

"But Carlos—"

Click.

I turn back to Talia, but she's across the street haggling over a finch paperweight.

Carlos's response is surprisingly heartbreaking. You'd think someone would forgive you for something you really didn't do. And even if you did do it, they would forgive you anyway. I'm a good person. People have done shit to me, and I've forgiven them. A lot of shit. Maybe it's a Latin thing. Or a man thing. Of course, it's a man thing. My dad was pissed at my mom for over twenty years for something that she only did after she was pissed at him for doing something to her first.[16]

Talia comes back, finch in hand. "What did Carlos say?"

"He didn't want to see me."

"Why not?"

"He's mad at me."

"Oh, okay. Let's head up to Vilcabamba, then."

Talia heads back to the bus terminal. I want to share with her how disappointed I am, but I'm embarrassed for being so sensitive. Why can't I be like Talia, who easily dismisses anyone who is angry at her whether their reasons are justified or not? Is it confidence? Indifference? Maturity? All of the above?

Yes, Dr. Kaufman, *of course* Carlos represents my dad, and my inner child is the one reacting, or, more accurately, overreacting. But this annoying inner child has ruled my inner playground and bullied away all the other inner children that are calmer, more mature, and able to handle situations like this in a mature fashion.

"Yeah, fuck him, fucking cocksucking cunty cocksucker!" I declare, hoping my excessive use of obscenities will send my inner child scurrying, hands over ears, into the nap room so as not to get in trouble with the teacher.

---

16 Never got the full story on that one, sorry.

26

LORDY LORDY LORDY

The ride to Vilcabamba is glorious. Ecuador is all greenery and loveliness, like Ireland, only without the sausage and bad complexions.

The moomlatz guesthouse is a lovely cabin nestled by a river. It's run by Petra, a Scandinavian woman who has managed to age remarkably gracefully—something about those button noses and blue eyes makes these Nordic types look young forever. I mean, look at Donald Sutherland. Okay, maybe not him, he looks a thousand. And he's not Nordic. But he *looks* Nordic. Maybe I'm thinking of Max von Sydow. Yes I am! Shit, he hasn't aged well either. Okay, one of the Bergmans. Or Harry Belafonte. But he's black. Black don't crack. Carla taught me that. Not a wrinkle. And don't try to tell me Morgan Freeman is wrinkled; he just has those weird nubbins on his skin. And his voice makes him sound old. He probably sounded like that when he was four.

Petra the beautiful offers us a fresh salad upon our arrival. We are hesitant—everyone knows that eating salads in Third World countries is a big no-no (fresh produce is often fertilized with such health-inducing items as human excrement), but Petra assures everyone that her vegetables are triple washed in filtered water and are safe for consumption, so we dive in, happy for a change in our Latin American diet, which so far has consisted of fried corn in various forms.[17]

Talia and I enjoy five servings of fresh veggies and head to the patio where we join a group of nicknamed Israelis: Rooli, Laffi, Idan, and Chezi (pronounced with a guttural, phlegm-releasing *ccchhh*).

Rooli is chubby and cherubic, Laffi is skeletal with a gargantuan nose and red curly hair, Chezi is tubby and giddy, and Idan is charming and perfect with soft honey skin, luscious Terrell lips, and large canoe-shaped green eyes. He's the one that I want.

He is also in the midst of relaying some animated anecdote.

"I thought my head was an orange, and I was like, shit, I'm an orange. I have no hands. I'm an orange!"

"You're an orange! You're an orange!" they all chant, laughing hysterically.

"That San Pedro is fucking insane!" Chezi exclaims.

"What happened to you in San Pedro?" Talia asks.

---

17 We've also sampled the occasional yucca, which is like a potato only with less taste, almost a negative taste, if you will, that literally sucks all other taste out of your mouth, somehow purifying your palate without sorbet-like perks.

"It's not a place, it's a cactus," Rooli explains. "It's the only reason people come to Vilcabamba."

"Really?" I say, "I thought it was the salads."

Idan laughs. Not an "I want to fuck you, you're so cute and funny" laugh, but one that conveys appreciation for my wit regardless. He continues to recap his San Pedro experience, which seems to have involved a river, laughy crying, and a lot of nudity.

Talia sits there, still unclear how a cactus can induce illusions of citrus.

"It's a psychedelic cactus," I tell her.

"A crazy, fucked-up, makes-you-want-to-laugh-and-pee-and-cry-and-kill-yourself cactus." Rooli adds.

"Oh." she says. "I've never taken drugs before. I thought they just made you tired."

How do I always choose travel partners dorkier than me? Maybe it makes me feel less dorky, or maybe I'm a lightweight and don't feel comfortable hanging out with true hard-core partiers and just want to dabble in the crazy life on occasion. Not that swallowing a cactus sounds crazy. Just painful.

Laffi lights up a joint.

"You mean you've never even smoked pot?"

Talia shakes her head.

"Come on, just take one puff," he tells her. "It's not going to kill you."

Where are the ABC Afterschool Special people with the placards on peer pressure when you need them?

"You going to take the San Pedro, Iris?" Idan asks.

"No, one bad shrooming experience was enough for me."

"Ooh, tell us, tell us!" they cry.

Talia is clearly uninterested, but I take no heed and launch into my shit village story. By the end of it, the guys are on the floor, and Talia sees me in a new, perplexed light.

"Is this your first trip after the army?" Idan asks, a new-found gleam in his eye.

"I backpacked through Asia a year ago."

"Wow! I hear the parties are the end of the world!" Rooli gushes.[18]

"It's true, Manali has the most amazing parties on earth."

"This is our first trip after the army," Laffi says, his nose crinkling as if it were about to cave in from its own enormity. He has potential to be cute, but I can't see any of his other features because of the massive turtle on his face masquerading as a sensory organ.

"How'd you afford two trips? Are your parents rich or something?" Rooli asks.

God bless Israeli directness. Some people find it abrasive, but I prefer knowing what's on someone's mind rather than discovering it via third party or gossip column.

The fact is, while my parents have always given me money when I needed it, my father raised me to work hard and never take anything for granted. *Anything.* Sometimes he went over the top. Like the time when I was 13 and came to New York to visit him at the bank where he worked. I was so excited by the prospect of making international calls

---

18 "and of the world": Hebrew slang for "amazing." Considering the very existence of turmoil-infused Israel is in constant peril, it's curious that we find terms like "end of the world" positive. Or understandable.

from his office for free that I dialed Talia in Israel, and we talked about David Bowie for over an hour. We had just launched into a harmonious rendition of "Modern Love" when my dad stepped out of his office and told me to hang up the phone. I belted out another "Terrifies me!" to Talia's "Church on time!' when Pop took the receiver from my hand, and informed me that I was to report back to the bank the next morning and work the entire day for free to "pay the bank back for my phone call." I guess he thought eight hours of my labor were worth $14, either that or my phone call to Israel was really fucking expensive. I do, however, credit him for endowing me with the same extreme code of ethics, and I have been overpaying my taxes ever since.

But I don't tell them all that.

"I paid for Asia by working as a waitress, and for this trip I used my bat mitzvah money. How about you guys?"

"We worked as male escorts."

I wait for the "Hahah, just kidding" to follow. It doesn't.

"Really?"

"Yeah, we slept with women for money. And made a lot of it."

Rooli and Laffi high-five. Idan smiles modestly, less like an escort, more like the brothel owner who only slept with select VIP clients.

Ah, the gender divide. As liberated as a woman is, as much as she fucks around and thinks it's okay, she would never announce to a group of strangers that she prostituted herself for a couple of months to catch the express train to San Pedroville. But when a man sells his penis to hundreds of desperate vaginas, he swings his used-up shlong from the mountaintops with pride. Is that a testament to how backward society is or to how stupid men are that they actually find whoring themselves out attractive?

Speaking of which, why do I find Idan much more attractive right now?

Just then an Australian woman in her 40s, her face etched by the sun, walks up to Idan, quietly kissing him on the forehead. Friend? Client?

"Chelsea," Idan coos, "these are our new friends, Talia and Iris."

"Hello, girls," she says in a sexy, Aussie accent.

"How'd you guys meet?" I ask. An odd first question, I know, but such information must be gathered as quickly and efficiently as possible.

"I met Chelsea in Cuzco," Idan replies. He gets up and grabs Chelsea a chair. They squeeze hands as she sits down. There is love there for sure, but it's of the quiet kind. The healthy kind that I'm supposed to want but can never have because there's too much fire burning inside me and I can't get past the "Oh no, the passion's gone!" phase that usually kicks in two weeks into the fuckfest that constitutes the beginning of a relationship.

Chelsea sips her tea and stares out into the wilderness. What's the appeal for Idan here? I have always admired guys who go for older women,[19] but Chelsea just looks boring. Maybe she's in the catatonic throes of a San Pedro hangover.

---

19. But only if the older women look nothing like the guys' mothers and don't possess any maternal qualities, because otherwise it's just creepy.

Or maybe Idan likes the quiet mature stable type. Shit. That definitely rules me out.

Of course, I'm forgetting one thing. Chelsea is blonde. Which to most readers outside the Middle East doesn't seem like anything special beyond the ole "blondes have more fun" cliché. But you must understand something—Israeli men have a particular obsession with blondes. It's like they are of a different species, which is why every pudgy German girl who can't get action from even the ugliest Aryan dork back home comes to a kibbutz for a few months and has her pick of the shag-hungry Israeli litter. In fact, a girl doesn't actually have to *be* blonde to get action in Israel. It's enough that her hair is some shade of taupe. Take Rina, this girl from high school, for example. Rina's face had an unmistakably rodenty quality to it, but her long hair was just light enough to deem her the class bombshell or *koosit*, as the term in Hebrew for hottie goes, which literally means vagina. Such is the forward thinking of my people.

Chelsea's hair, on the other hand, is pure blonde—golden fields of sunflowery goodness kind of blonde—and combined with her Aussie serenity she offers Idan a tranquil life, full of koala milk and understanding. All I have to offer is a tortured soul and hormonal overload. And love. I can offer love. An enormous amount of unbridled love. I have so much love to give it feels like a toxin running through my veins that needs to be flushed out.

I don't mean to say that love is toxic; it's just that my love doesn't have an outlet. And it's been running amok in my blood for so long without a purpose that it has fermented and grown bitter that it's still trapped inside my small, confused body, desperate to find a mate that will release it from its interminable prison.

"Are you okay, Iris?" Idan asks, perplexed. "You're staring at Chelsea's scalp."

"What? Oh sorry, I got lost there for a minute, all those beautiful yellow follicles, they're mesmerizing."

Chelsea smiles, takes Idan's hand, and leads him back to their little wooden cottage for some kangaroo inspired copulation. There is something beautiful about the way they walk together, and I suddenly feel a sharp pang in my chest, not just yearning for Idan but more for that sense of intimacy that two people can share—something I have never experienced. Beforehand, I couldn't be in a relationship because I was too scared of sex, but now I can't be in a relationship because all I know how to do is *have* sex, and the minute it gets more intimate than that I freak out.

I should have started my own escort service.

"What do you want to do now?" Talia asks, jolting me out of my hole of identi-pity.

"I don't know. I thought we could just hang out and relax."

Talia does not like this idea. I never thought of her as the antsy type. I thought she was the perfect person with whom to spend catatonic time in exotic locations, but after the Inca Trail I realize I was wrong. About a lot of things. But I'm slowly accepting that fact with grace and dignity. I think.

Talia goes to talk to Nordic wonder at the reception desk about various activities. She returns, not with activity pamphlets but Turbogaz herself. Goddammit.

"Look who I found!" Talia says, ecstatic.

"Hey, Pazit. What are you doing here?"

That didn't sound as accusatory as you think. Honestly.

"Huaraz was snowed in, so I came here instead."

"I told Pazit she should join us for the rest of our trip," Talia says.

I am stunned. Talia smiles, unaware of yet another backpacker faux pas she has committed by inviting someone else along without consulting her travel partner first.

I will work through my shit. I will work through my shit.

"Oh," I say with a forced smile. "Okay."

Just then Idan and Chelsea return, a gizzy glow about them. My usual smitten symptoms kick into gear: palpitations. Stomach ulcer. Rectal tightening. That's a new one. I've never felt a tightening in my rectum before, not this kind. Wow. Painful yet cool. Maybe I was wrong about my whole no-anal-sex policy.

Why is Idan so different? I wonder if it's his unavailability that I find safe and appealing. God, I wish I weren't so self-aware every millisecond of the day. The cacophony of my brain is overwhelming.

Maybe hanging out with Turbogaz and engaging in more nature-minded activities (as opposed to worrying about my intimacy issues and staring at men who are obviously taken) is exactly what I need. Maybe that's why people spend time walking in the mountains for no reason—to quiet their minds. Maybe God is telling me something.

"You want to go for a little hike?" Pazit asks us. "There's a beautiful path along the river, it's only five or six miles."

God can't be telling me to do *that*. That's just crazy.

"Oh, I'd love to, but I have a massage scheduled for 2:00 p.m."

"You do?" Talia says.

"Yeah, I . . . uh . . . scheduled it . . . earlier."

"Oh. Okay," Talia says, once again void of any disappointment.

"Have fun!" I say, rushing to the front desk to schedule my already scheduled massage.

"Yes, of course, we have an amazing masseuse," Scandaqueen gushes, "with the most beautiful massage room in the world." She points to a small hill in the distance. At the top of the hill is a small massage table. Wow. She's not kidding. I sooo made the right choice on this one. "Our masseuse will meet you up there in fifteen minutes. Just undress, and get on the table. Nobody can see anything from down below, so feel free to take all your clothes off."

I arrive out of breath, but the serenity of the hilltop calms me instantly. The air is clean, the breeze gentle, and the pristine sheets on the massage table soft and welcoming, everything an uptight Jew could ask for!

I take off my clothes and lie on the table, head down, my white butt cheeks deflecting the hot sun back to the heavens.

I hear footsteps up the hill. I try to relax my body so the masseuse doesn't detect my un-Zenlike state and not want to work on me. Kind of like how my mom always cleans the house the day before the maid comes.

The masseuse doesn't say a word. No hello, what a nice white ass you have, nothing. Which is fine by me. Nothing worse than a chatty masseuse. Or hair stylist. Or waitress. The list goes on.

A bottle squirts, lavender fills the air, and the journey begins.

Gentle yet firm, strong yet sensual, the masseuse's hands work and listen, releasing the anxiety in my neck, the fear in my hands, the agony in my stomach. My tears flow slowly and rhythmically. We stay silent the entire time, inhaling and exhaling in perfect harmony.

By the time Magic Hands reaches my scalp, my nose shmarf is dribbling through the massage table head-hole, but I don't care—I've never felt better. It's as if a white light has been beamed throughout my body and cleansed the inner core of my being.

The massage comes to a close with a little chime. I want to lie there forever, but I don't because that would be inconsiderate and creepy. So I sit up, ready to take in my savior. The sun is blinding. The only thing I can make out is a sea of golden follicles.

Okay, Idan, I get it now. I totally, totally get it.

27

WHY DO YOU ASK?

Scheisse! I just realized something awful—it's been two weeks since I called my mother.

I rush to the reception phone where none other than dreamboat Idan is on the phone with his own mother. So happy he's not fucking Chelsea right now. He smiles and gives me the Israeli sign for "just a sec." (Take note: The same sign means "Fuck you!" in Italy, so make sure you don't ask to delay any activities when visiting Rome.)

You can tell so much about a man by the way he talks to his mother. Idan was clearly a good kid, the kind who ate his vegetables and helped his mother clean the house while his brother jacked off and listened to King Crimson.

Idan hangs up and steps aside. I don't want him to leave. He doesn't. Somehow his just standing there while I dial my mom doesn't feel weird.

My mom answers before the first ring is complete.

"Hey, Ima!"

"Hey, honey, how are you?" my mom replies with unusual calmness. I was fully expecting the meltdown shriek-show almost-had-a-heart-attack why-didn't-you-call? shpiel.

"I'm great, Ima. Weren't you worried?"

"Why would I be worried? You're with Talia."

Whoa, momma be all normal and shit. Something's not right.

"Are you still in Peru?" She asks.

"No, we're in Ecuador now."

"Fantastic! How's Talia?"

"She's good, she's out hiking. How's Porsche?"

"You own a Porsche?" Idan mouths, baffled.

"He's my cat," I mouth back. "Ima? You there?"

"Yes, yes, I'm here."

"How is Porsche doing?"

"He's . . . fine."

My mother was never a good liar.

"Ima, is Porsche sick?"

"What? I can't hear you very well."

My heart starts to pound, the room begins to spin.

"Ima, is Porsche dead?"

"Why do you ask?"

"IMA!"

She takes a long drag of her cigarette. "Yes."

"When?"

"Three weeks ago."

"Porsche died *three weeks* ago?! Why didn't you tell me?!"

"I didn't want to upset you."

"Too late!"

The tears begin. Idan puts his arm around me.

"Don't let this ruin your trip, sweetheart."

"That was my cat, Ima. For fifteen years."

"I know, honey, I know. It was hard for me too. Try and have a good time, okay? I love you."

"I love you too."

I hang up. Idan hugs me tight.

"That cat went through a lot with me," I mumble into Idan's chest. "He wasn't the sharpest tool in the shed, but he was there during the worst of times."

"Why didn't she tell you?" he asks.

"Well, my mother has major issues with bad news and death, especially bad news involving death. Her parents both died within a few months of each other when she was very young. She has never visited their graves and as a rule doesn't set foot in cemeteries, ever. She believes that, if bad news is not spoken, it never happened. She is also an avid student of the related school of thought that believes if you don't go to a doctor you will never get sick, which is third cousin to the school that scary diseases will disappear if ignored or not treated. I literally had to threaten a hunger strike once just to get her to have a mammogram, which ended up revealing a growth that had to be removed *twice* by a very competent yet arrogant doctor in Haifa and his trusty Arab-Israeli intern, Osama. Osama hit on me several times during our stay at Haifa General, but I was too busy worrying about my mother's health to entertain anything else. Not to mention it's kinda weird dating somebody who has seen and touched your mother's breasts."[20]

---

20 You were thinking I was going to say it's weird dating somebody named Osama, but I'm much more evolved than that.

Idan laughs. Does he admire my ability to make jokes even during my time of painful mourning, or does he think I hide behind humor to mask my pain and insecurity like one of those annoying stand-up comics who are always "on"?

❧

Miami, 1983.

The height of my parents' divorce. In an attempt to find some joy during this volatile time, my mother called her friends in Miami, Mauricio and Lana Alhadeff, a sweet Cuban couple who had a buoyant boy my age named Jacob. Mauricio was one of the few people on the planet who actually had a heart of gold. Lana was an equally sweet woman with a hairdo that involved a side part and two perfectly swirled tendrils.

The Alhadeffs were our go-to companions for our annual Disney World/Epcot excursions. They were also aware that my family situation had deteriorated substantially as of late and realized that my mother and I needed a more potent diversion than a replica of Cairo or some pervert in a Mickey Mouse costume. And so they suggested we join them on their annual cruise from Miami to the Bahamas and Finger Islands. I had never been on a cruise, but I knew from *The Love Boat* that it was fun and involved a chatty bartender, lots of good food, and shuffleboard. I was so excited!

We flew to Miami and met the Alhadeffs at the port. It was like a dream, walking hand in hand with mommy up the long walkway and into the luxury cruise liner. The smiling crew greeted us as we prepared to traverse the ocean toward unknown lands with funny names.

Once inside, we followed the Alhadeffs down the carpeted hallway, stopping by their room first.

"I'm going to walk Ruthie and Iris to their room," said Mauricio, always the gentleman. Jacob jumped on his massive red velvet bed in glee.

Alhadeff looked at our tickets. "Follow me."

We walked down the hallway and down the stairs. A lot of stairs. Five flights of stairs to be precise.

"Are we staying underwater?" I asked, confused.

"No, of course not, honey. We just couldn't afford the expensive rooms upstairs."

"Oh. Okay."

The doors on this floor were a lot closer to each other, like dozens of little broom closets in a row. Mauricio opened ours to reveal a broom closet. Which happened to have two narrow bunk beds and a tiny window dangerously close to sea level. My mother smiled at me, embarrassed. I felt bad that she felt bad, so I ran to the bunk bed and jumped on it, promptly thwacking my head on the super low ceiling.

Mauricio smiled through his pity. "Meet you in an hour for dinner. You're going to love the food. It's fantastic!"

The ship tooted its massive horn, triggering my excitement once again.

"Let's take a walk around!" my mother said desperately. Brilliant idea.

We ascended the stairs back to civilization and the entertainment deck. The nightclub had a sign on the door that read "TALENT SHOW 8 PM." My heart skipped a beat. I wanted nothing more than to go on stage that night and do something of talent, though I had no idea what that talent was.

My mom suggested I do some accents. Those were always a big hit when company was over. "Do the Spanish woman, Iris!" they would order, and my 5-year-old ass would launch into a flawless imitation of a woman speaking amazingly Spanish-sounding gibberish. "Do the tour guide in Rome!" they'd squeal, and I would imitate the woman who took us on a tour of the ruins with a pitch-perfect rendition of her line, "This was marble they brought in from Carrara."

"Say 'Carrara' again, Iris! Say it! SAY IT!"

"Carrrrarrrra!" my little voice would squeak, rolling the R in pure Italian bravado with the cuteness of a first grader. The company would marvel at my skills. My dad's friend Ron the painter said, "She's a firecracker, this one. She's like a radio!" which apparently made complete sense to the adults but not to me. I was not a radio. Why would he say that?

My mother put my name down on the talent contest sign-up list. There were already ten acts before me, but I was in prime eleventh position. I couldn't wait to do my accents for the crowd! Neither could my mom, who said we should hurry to the restaurant and have dinner before eight.

The dining room was an elaborate festival of ice sculptures and decadence, long tables of obesity-inducing foods displayed in the most tempting manner possible. We filled our plates to the brim and joined the Alhadeffs, who had already managed to fill two plates each.

Just as I dug into the Caesar salad–artichoke hearts–flank steak–baked potato–brussel sprouts–fettuccine alfredo–french fries–chocolate cake–lemon meringue–salmon in cream dill sauce–cherry tomatoes with mozzarella balls on my plate, the ship veered to the left. Dramatically. I held on to my plate, immediately feeling a pang of nausea. That's all it took—one veer left, and my stomach went into puke mode. Another veer to the right. The food swirled in front of me. The Alhadeffs, in contrast, kept downing their meal voraciously, using the movement of the ship as their personal digestive aid.

"Ima, I'm going to throw up," I said.

"Okay, let's go back to the room."

"Aren't you going to eat?" Mauricio asked, concerned. "The mashed potatoes with bacon are fantastic, and the steak couldn't be juicier!"

"Yeah, this creamed corn is awesome!" Jacob chimed in, several creamed kernels stuck to his cheek.

"Ima, I'm really going to throw up. *Now.*"

Ima grabbed my hand and rushed me down into the dungeon. The veering had worsened. I rushed into the tiny bathroom and hurled for what seemed like an eternity, then heaved air for another eternity, before finally crawling into my bunk.

The captain announced over the PA system that a storm was approaching, one so strong that we would have to skip the Finger Islands and head straight for the Bahamas.

By that time it was already 8:30. No talent show for me. I cried quietly, my body sliding to and fro along the plastic mattress, the waves crashing up against our tiny porthole.

&

I've finally managed to compose myself, post-Porsche news, but am having a harder time releasing myself from Idan's manly embrace. So I force a few more sobs that send me further into his torso until Chelsea suddenly rounds the corner.

"Is everything all right, Iris?" she asks, taking Idan's hand into her lavender grasp.

"Her cat died," Idan says.

"Oh, I'm so sorry to hear that. Why don't you join us for a little bite?"

That would be weird.

"Yes, join us!" Idan says, taking my hand.

Then again, weird experiences are my specialty.

೪

Idan and I sit on the porch as Chelsea brings out a delicious platter of goat cheese, tomatoes, olives, and freshly baked bread. As we eat quietly, I come to several realizations, some related to my current situation, others related to my other current situation:

1. Unrequited, one-sided, imaginary love is unsatisfying.
2. Really peaceful people are unnerving.
3. I am still deeply threatened by Turbogaz.
4. My eyebrows are nothing to write home about either.

Who am I kidding? Idan is in love with this golden goddess, and I'm wasting my time and my heart being here. I need to move forward on my healing journey, not rip new holes in my emotional parachute. It's time to go urban and take the girls to Quito—a hikeless refuge where Pazit will feel out of place, I will accumulate some self-esteem and mojo, and most importantly, I will finally return to my prime position as entertainer, haggler, and best friend.

28

OPEN LOS OJOS

Sorry I haven't written or called. I've been stuck inside the bathroom on a bus to Quito for the last eight hours, all because some Jew-hating Norwegian lied to me about how clean her salads were. My stomach has been taken hostage by contaminated tomato terrorists that have unleashed a nuclear attack on my innards. It is as if an alien were playing hopscotch in my stomach, wearing cleated footwear.[21]

Shit, vomit, shit. Shit, vomit, cough. Hack, spit, shit. Repeat. All while trying to balance myself over the toilet seat without touching it. By the time we get to Quito, I'm so weak and dehydrated that my limp body has to be carried off the bus by Pazit and Talia.

"Take us to the nearest hospital, please!" Talia tells a cab driver with quiet authority.

---

21 Let me apologize for the heightened frequency of body function stories in the last few chapters, please know that my shit does not stink and my vomit is sexy and lavender-colored.

He stares at them blankly. I am fading dangerously fast, so I kick into gear.

"*Emergéncia,*" I moan to the driver in my weakened hazy state.

He doesn't budge, a clueless look on his face.

"*Emergéncia!*" I say more emphatically.

The girls chime in: "*Emergéncia! Emergéncia!! Emergéncia!!!*"

We might as well be speaking Sanskrit.

I moan in pain, the stomach alien now channeling Savion Glover.

"*Emergéncia!*" I repeat nine more times, intermittently drooling and fading in and out of consciousness. One more time and I'm done. "*EMERGÉNCIA!*"

The driver tilts his head, dog-like. Suddenly his eyes light up. "Ah! *Emergencía!*" he cries, with a slightly different emphasis. "*Claro!* Emergen*ciiiiiii*aaaa*!! Hospital! Inmediatamente!*"

I mentally thwack the idióta/idiotá in the head with my shoe and we drive off.

 es

Upon arrival at the *Emergenciiiiíaaaa* Room, I am whisked away on a stretcher, Talia and Pazit following close behind. I can barely make sense of what's going on and fear that it will be hours before I receive any care, but several minutes later blood is drawn from my anemic arm. Soon thereafter a very sweet doctor arrives, one with full command of the English language. He speaks with a strong, sexy Scottish accent. He tells me he's an intern on some Third World fellowship of sorts and my medication is on its way.

My blood work comes back teeming with fraggles. I expect to be offered a bed until I am cured, but Braveheart says there is no need, i.e., there's no room for any patient not in need of a heart transplant. He hands me a bottle of pills and escorts us outside, where we slide into a cab and head toward the moomlatz Buena Villa Guesthouse.

Talia and Pazit carry me to a small room on the second floor and plop me onto the bed. I am still in a great deal of pain, but the bodily fluid ejectors seem to be taking a little siesta.

The attention I'm getting from the girls is making me uncomfortable. Maybe it's because I've always spent my energy worrying about other people, no doubt to take my attention off my own crap. Nevertheless, this guilt prompts me to mumble through my semi-conscious stupor, "I'm okay, guys. You go out and have fun. I'll be fine resting."

"What's that, Iris? I can't understand what you're saying," Pazit says wiping a bit of saliva off my chin.

"Don't stay here because of me. Go out and have fun!"

To which Talia and Pazit reply, "Are you sure?" as they run off to find deals on cheap socks and portable sinks.[22]

My eyes close as the place goes quiet. I am alone.

I don't know how much time has passed, but it's clear that I have begun to lose all corporeal sensation. People talk about

---

22 Etiquette note: "Are you sure?" should always be delivered a minimum of two times to ensure the other party even remotely believes you are considering his or her desires. Anything less is unacceptable and embarrassing.

"out of body" experiences, but this is a no-body experience; it's like I have nothing but a head with a horribly alert mind that is acutely aware of its vessel's rapid deterioration. I am fading into dangerously dehydrated oblivion, and it is clear to me that if someone doesn't come help me very soon I will die.

Some parents survive the horror of their children's death, but my mother would not. She's too fragile. Why does she deserve a daughter who chooses to eat salads in Third World countries? Who leaves her mother alone to study in Bumblefuck, New England, and take her only three months off to roam South America instead of going back home for a family visit? What kind of monster am I?

Speaking of monsters, where the fuck are Talia and Pazit? I can't believe they just left me like this. That's not a healthy boundary, that's plain sociopathic.

Oh, here they are, coming up the stairs. About time. They're going to come in and see me and call the hospital again, at which point Braveheart will kick a transplant candidate off his bed to make room for me so I can be grateful and write a big check for the new Organ Smuggling Wing or at the very least donate a soda machine for the lobby.

The door opens. It's not Talia or Pazit but a tall Ecuadorian woman with two rolls of toilet paper in her hand. "Help!" I yell, "I need to get to a hospital!" but she doesn't even look at me. It dawns on me that no sound is coming out of my mouth. That bullshit film cliché when people can't scream for help? That bullshit cliché is happening to me right now.

I attempt to move my eyebrows in an urgent communicative fashion, but have no control over my facial features either. I want to cry. Can't do that either. Shit, maybe I am crying, and don't even know it.

The woman turns to look at me, not reacting to the fact that I'm lying here corpse-like with my eyes darting around the room like Hannibal Lecter. She puts the toilet paper rolls on the dresser and leaves.

If only Idan were here, caressing my numb face, staring at me with his beautiful green eyes, his girlfriend rubbing my shoulders and cleaning up my fecal matter. But he's not here. Nobody is. I am going to die alone in a moomlatz guesthouse in Ecuador. God, this fucking sucks.

My eyes are closing again. In keeping with bullshit film cliché form, a sense of peace washes over me, that peace that comes before death. Which is not really peaceful. It's more like acceptance, I guess. An acceptance that stems from the realization that fighting death would only make it more painful. There is nothing I can do—I am here alone, and I am going to die alone in the next few minutes. I am filled with the serenity of not having to worry about anything for the first time in my life. My eyelids descend for the last time, and I fade to black.

❧

"Iris! Iris, wake up!"

Someone is shaking my shoulder. I moan. My eyes are locked shut. I can hear Talia and Pazit whisper frantically, as if they feared speaking too loud would wake me up. Isn't that the point?

"We need to call an ambulance!" Talia says.

More whispering.

"We can't bring her back to that hospital; they're the ones who told her to come back here in the first place," Talia says.

That's my girl. Keep the guy whose medical training was limited to playing Operation on the streets of Edinburgh away from me.

"Let's call the Israeli embassy," Pazit suggests.

I smile (internally). She's not so bad, this Turbogaz lassie. Shit, now they're leaving. Again. Why does it take two girls to make a phone call? What if I stop breathing?

The toilet flushes. Whew, one of them has stayed.

"Damn," Pazit mumbles, unable to find the toilet paper.

If only I could tell her the cleaning woman left it on the dresser. She'll have to do a drip and dry. We should all have such problems right now.

Talia races back into the room, breathing heavily.

"Israeli embassy is closed."

"Shit."

"What do we do?"

"The American embassy?"

"Good idea!"

Talia runs out again. Pazit finds the toilet paper and goes in for a second sitting.

More stair racing. Talia flies back in. "They're closed too!"

What the hell is going on? It's 3:00 p.m. on a Tuesday!

"What are we going to do?" Pazit asks.

"I don't know. I'll try again."

"I'll come with you."

They finally return, victory in their step.

"The German embassy is sending a doctor!" Talia announces.

When Jews call the Germans for help, you know you're in trouble. Pazit throws a wet rag on my face. I try not to think where she got it. I just enjoy the sensation of gloriously cold drops of water strolling down my face.

ဢ

The doctor arrives within the hour. God bless the Germans. (Hey, I've moved on. Forgive, but don't forget, as the saying goes.) He prods me in odd places, at one point pushing my stomach all the way to my spine. My eyes bolt open. I wish they had stayed closed. The man hovering over me looks less like a physician and more like an extra from *Kojak*. He's wearing a ribbed green turtleneck, orange blazer, and massive tinted Chanel sunglasses. His dark burgundy toupée is almost square shaped, like those old action figures whose hair came in plastic pieces you could pop on and off.

He looks at the bottle of medication. "Who gave her this?"

"The hospital."

"Idiots. It's the wrong medication. If she doesn't get fluids in her system, she will die very shortly."

Told you!

So why the hell is nobody shoving fluids down my throat?

Presto. Doctor Zhivago pulls my head off the pillow, and the sweet taste of fake cantaloupe hits my tongue. Talia takes my new, correct medication, and Captain Steubing heads off to catch Julie on Deck B before she slides into a crack-ridden stupor.

29

DONATE NOW!!

Within five days, I am up and in full control of my muscles and vocal cords. Talia catches me looking at the Colombia section of our *Lonely Planet*.

"You're kidding, right?" she asks.

"What do you mean? We wanted to go to Colombia next, remember?"

"We're not going *anywhere*. You almost died a few days ago! You should go back to Providence."

"What? (And let you travel with Pazit without me?) No way."

"Iris—"

"No. Talia, I'm serious. Not finishing this trip is going to be more detrimental to my health than any mystery ailment could ever be."

She looks at me, and for the first time she realizes this trip is more than just a random Latin romp for me. She doesn't say anything in response. She is aware of my profound inner sadness but has nothing to say—not because she doesn't want to, but because it's a blip that doesn't amply register on her emotional map.

I finally know. What I want, that is. It's not for Talia to want to spend more time with me, or for her to need me more than I need her, or for her to tell everyone that I'm her best friend. What I want is to be seen by that one person on the planet who makes me feel less lonely, not by his or her company or a few laughs but by the fact that they truly understand me and my pain, my entire being, the stuff that makes sense and the stuff that doesn't. Maybe that's true friendship. Maybe that's true love.

It's a lot to demand of another human being, I guess. I know now that Talia can't feel my pain because my kind of pain is completely beyond her field of comprehension, as is her ability to empathize or sympathize. (I always confuse the two, but I know they're both important.) The way I see it, some of us tear up when we see those UNICEF commercials on TV, some of us realize how hungry we are and go make ourselves a sandwich, some of us cringe and change the channel, and some of us just stare at the screen blankly, waiting for our favorite program to come back on.

COLOMBIA

30

LOCO-MOTION

Colombia is a dangerous place, especially now. It is currently defined as being in a "severe state of emergency," a state I know well. You might be asking—why would one willingly go to a place in such a state if he or she were not a drug dealer or aid worker? I don't know. You're asking someone who paid to look for a dead guy in a river and shat out her spleen after eating salad. Maybe my experience knocking on death's door and actually hanging out in death's kitchen eating brie and Wasa crackers has given me an unjustified sense of bravery and immortality.

Our first stop, San Agustin, is known among the muchilleros for its horseback riding. I've only been horseback riding once, in Yosemite, when I was 12. It was there that I learned the meaning of sore poon.

Our Colombian horse wrangler presents each of us with two choices of horse—*calma* and *poco calma*. Talia and Pazit choose the *calmas*. Me? I point to another, larger horse tied behind the wrangler's truck that's in the midst of some manic kickboxing frenzy. "That one!" I say. "I want that one!"

Clinto the cowboy looks at the horse and shakes his head. "*No, no, esto es loco. LOCO.*"

"*Loco* is okay. Trust me, I know."

He makes a horrible face that involves buggy eyes and several chin and forehead crunches. He unties the horse, whispering something into its ear that's either "Relax" or "This idiot wants to ride you." Either way, Loco calms down, and the wrangler helps me onto the saddle, utilizing a bit too much of my crotch area for support. He then hops up onto his personal black stallion, and we begin our ride up a horse-shit-ridden trail into the mountains. Huge pyramids of poop one after the other. Sometimes I wish I could just crouch and take a massive industrial-sized shit in the middle of the street, a shit that would start with cringing and end with a roar so loud that the shit itself would be scared shitless, trembling there on the ground, staring back up at my butt, begging for re-entry.

The trail is narrow, so we ride in single file, Clinto in the lead and Loco and I bringing up the rear. We're going slow enough to take photos of the beautiful San Agustin views. I don't know why Loco got a bad rap. I'm so tired of people looking at us feistier types as crazy or unstable. Yeah, we have our moments, but we are fully capable of relaxing. Just don't tell us to relax. Or not to worry. Or calm down. We will do it in our own time, right, Loco? I pat him on the neck (or what seems to be his neck—horse bodies are weird—I can't really tell what's what). Loco smiles back. Bottom line is, all we crazy people need is understanding. It's the people who look at us funny that make us crazy.

My small display of affection endows Loco with added confidence. He trots up to Talia's Calma and nuzzles her ass/lower torso area. That's why I love animals: no bullshit, direct contact, straight to the penetration point. Maybe it's better that we as humans have "evolved"; otherwise the streets would be filled with men running up to passing vaginas, sniffing and smell-checking, before pursuing any sort of verbal contact (whose only goal is to lead to more aggressive sniffing that will hopefully lead to copulation within a minimal time frame anyway).

Loco nuzzles Calma's tail out of the way to get better nose-to-butt contact, shaking Talia off balance.

"Whoa! Iris, stop that!"

"Me? I'm not doing anything! It's not my fault my horse wants to shtoop your horse."

"Well, your horny horse is going to get me killed!"

By now we're pretty high up and the trail is narrow as ever. Maybe she's right.

LEWD INTERLUDE #8:
(the previous 6 were too offensive to print).

I hate getting mass e-mails, especially ones that threaten sudden death if I don't forward love and kindness and femme power to fourteen other friends within the hour.

But this friend had never sent me mass e-mails before, so I figured I had better heed the "must read" subject line.

The e-mail informed me that a man in some state in the Pacific Northwest was recently killed by a horse, the moment of death captured on video by the man's boyfriend. Somehow the video wound up in police custody. Shortly thereafter, the police released a warning that while having sex with large animals in that state was legal, having sex with small animals was not. (Finally we small creatures were getting the protection we deserved.)

The video was attached to the e-mail. And yes, I clicked on it.

Before me appeared a man. A naked man with piercings on his penis. And a horse. With a hard-on. (Mind you, I'm a city girl. I'd never seen a horse's hard-on, and God help me it's terrifying.) How the naked man got the horse aroused in the first place is a separate question to be contemplated later. Please understand that my curiosity was morbid, not sexual. Sex with farm animals doesn't really do it for me. Sure, I can understand why some of my soldier friends stationed in the boonies occasionally found comfort watching cows fuck, but that was different.

The man positioned himself behind the horse. I figured this was the moment that he would penetrate the horse. No such luck. Instead, he then moved in *front* of the horse and guided the horse *into him*. Now this was revolutionary, or as the police stated in their press release "not usual."

"The horse is *not* going to fuck you!" I yelled at the screen. "Stop kidding yourself—you're not a horse!"

But the man knew better than I. He guided the horse's ballistic missile a half an inch into his butt. The horse did not look happy. Not that I'm an expert gauge of equine facial expressions, but you could just tell. Naked man forced it in another inch. That had to hurt. Then again, this guy looked like a pro. Who knows what household appliances he'd already thrust in there. For all I knew, he'd already had sex with actual ballistic missiles. Another inch. Wow. The horse turned to the camera for a moment, shaking its head in disapproval, and in a single breath thrust his *entire* ninety-foot penis into the man's ass. I screamed. The man grunted and fell to the ground, dead.

I had never seen anyone die on film before, and it was a harrowing experience. I closed the browser window, repulsed at myself for having watched such a vile piece of snuff, then immediately forwarded it to a few friends and edgier family members.

❧

I thank the video for educating me on equine foreplay, which is why I'm not surprised when Loco ignores my heed and nudges Calma more aggressively.

"He just wants to get in front of you," I tell Talia, who is both pale and annoyed, an unappealing combination.

"Well, how is he going to do that?" she asks.

"I don't know, Talia. I'm not a horse whisperer."

"A what?"

"Doesn't matter. Just pull over. Let me pass."

Talia pulls Calma toward the mountainside. Loco brushes past her and Pazit, trotting straight up the line up to Clinto.

"*Hola!*" I say to Clinto, who's obviously impressed at how I'm handling his schizoid horse. He picks up our pace to a trot. Calma and Poco Calma come up gingerly from behind, trotting in perfect unison with their master. Loco, however, doesn't budge, and we fall back to the rear again.

"Come on, Loco, don't embarrass me now."

I give him a slight nudge with my heels. You'd think I shoved razor blades into his sides because he lets out a loud *whowhwowa* worthy of an Ebola-ridden hyena and accelerates into a gallop, shoving past the entire group and down the trail at an alarming speed.

I am screaming now, holding on to Loco for dear life. His hooves sporadically slip off the precipice. Talia and Pazit are screaming too, which I'm sure Loco interprets as encouragement. Clinto is yelling "*Parale! Parale!*" but parale isn't fucking working. We're flying so fast I have no choice but to bury my face in Loco's chin/upper back/shoulder. The only way I can avoid catapulting off his body is by digging my feet into the stirrups as firmly as possible, but the stirrups are flailing, and my feet keep digging into Loco's ribs, which is sending mixed messages and only exacerbating the situation.

Maybe I need to stop fighting it. This horse is gonna do what it wants to do, and instead of trying to control it, I should let it control me. I should trust Loco because trust is a beautiful thing. And I'm probably going to be thrown off the mountain momentarily anyway.

My anxious grasp on Loco's neck becomes a firm hug. My feet relax into his body, and before I know it our bodies become one. (No potential snuff video here, this union is spiritual.) My back arches (still not sexual—get your mind out of the gutter) as we cut through the wind. Clinto and the girls' frantic voices fade in the distance until it's just Loco and me racing through the ether. I could swear we non-sexually come at the same time. Such an orgasm does exist; it's a feeling of pure joy that shudders through your body with such force that you cannot deny that at that brief moment you and the world are complete.

$$\mathcal{C}\mathcal{O}$$

Back at the ranch, I bask in the girls' admiration. Clinto is also impressed, though you can't tell by the facial-muscle fiesta transpiring on his face. He grabs my crotch, helps me off Loco, and drags him to his exiled location behind the truck. Loco and I gaze into each other's eyes for one last magical moment, knowing that we shared something special, a horse-human interaction that was astoundingly intimate, totally legal, comfortably non-invasive, and undoubtedly transcendent.

31

HOP IN!

Bogotá. If the city had a welcome mat, it would be made of toxic spikes, what with its gunpoint muggings, criminals dressed as cops who drug and then rob you, and actual cops who do the same thing.

Our guesthouse is in the worst part of town, but it's moomlatz and blessed with a double-steel bulletproof door. The terror here is palpable. It's in the air, on the ground, in the streets, and, most important, right in front of the guesthouse, where last night a young Israeli was stabbed for not relinquishing his fleece jacket to a knife-wielding gang.

Yossi: This is my Patagonia, Jorge. Mine! I don't care that you have a knife. My name is Yossi, and it's my fleece, and I'm keeping it. No, I will not "hand it over." I'm Israeli, we don't just "hand things over," asshole. Ow. That knife hurts, man. Cut it out. Did you just chop off my arm? Yeah, nice try, you're still not getting my fleece. Oh, I see you're chopping off my other arm. Think you're all smart and violent, huh? Well, guess what, now I'm sleeveless and sleeveless fleece vests are so 1996, so hahahahaha!

I'm happy to report that another Brown *internacional* named Guillermo lives in Bogotá, and he has several perks:

1. He's hot.
2. I want to sleep with him.
3. He doesn't hate my guts.

Talia is skeptical of that third perk, but I assure her he is no Carlos and will actually be happy to hear from me. One positive phone call later, turns out I am right! Guillermo even wants to "show us around." Heck, I might even get laid tonight!

"I will pick you up at 7:00 p.m., and take you to Zona Rosa. They have a great club there, and we can drink and dance all night!"

Awesome! Even Pazit is excited. I give him our address and say how psyched my girlfriends and I are for a fun night out.

A long pause follows.

Guillermo apologizes, mumbling that he's not sure tonight is going to work out.

I'm confused. "Was it the three girls? Is that too much?"

"No, of course not," he assures me. "I'm Latin. I love women!"

"So what is it?"

"It's just that . . . you guys are staying in a very danger-ous neighborhood. I've never been there, and I certainly won't start now. Even taxis don't go to that neighborhood."

Another awkward pause. I don't know what to say. This whole situation is a little ridiculous, not to mention a real bummer. I can feel Talia and Pazit bonding over my failure. The situation must be salvaged. I change tactics.

"We were all really excited to go out with you, Guill-ermo, and it's not just cuz you're hot. But that's okay, I understand. I guess the girls and I will just take off our skimpy little outfits and haul our horny promiscuous Israeli butts back to our room for the night and touch our—"

"No! No! It's okay, I'll come pick you guys up, not a problem."

"Are you sure?" I only ask once, this situation too fragile to risk another.

"Yes, of course, of course, I'll bring my friend Pedro with me."

I give the girls a thumbs-up. Talia and Pazit squeal excitedly.

His only condition is that once he arrives we get in the car *immediately* and not linger so as to avoid attract-ing attention, i.e., carjacking, kidnapping, extortion, and/or death. A reasonable request by all accounts.

The girls and I race upstairs and get dressed. I had

forgotten how good it feels to go party. I'm feeling so amped I even loan Pazit a cute purple top and some tweezers.

At 7:00 p.m. sharp we take our position behind the metal door and wait for Guillermo's car. A bright red Mercedes (stealthy choice, my friend) comes flying down the road at a ridiculous speed. His chubby friend Pedro sports a rich man's disheveled mop of dirty blonde hair. (Rich people somehow have different headmops than poor people. There is a qualitative difference between the *I can't find a job my family is broke they need me* disheveled mop and the *I don't need a job my parents are billionaires they just bought me a boat* disheveled mop.)

Guillermo is visibly nervous as he begins to slow down. We unbolt the metal guesthouse door and rush toward the car. He unlocks the doors, and we start piling into the backseat, but he starts driving away before Talia can close the door. "Wait!" I cry.

Guillermo keeps driving. Talia's leg is left dangling out the door.

"We have to move!" he orders, swerving left and right to avoid potential gunfire.

We try to pull Talia into the vehicle but with little success. Her left leg is three seconds away from getting lobbed off by a telephone pole.

"Guillermo, *STOP* THE CAR!!" we all scream.

His eyes dart around nervously. He keeps going.

"GUILLERMO!"

He stops just in time, and we yank Talia into the vehicle

and slam the door. Guillermo jets off at the speed of light toward the safe enclave of his wealthy brethren uptown.

We drive the whole way in silence, Guillermo and Pedro oozing resentment for having to venture for us to the dark side, and we for feeling like the second-class citizens they've turned us into.

The music at this club better be worth it.

ↄ

We follow Guillermo toward the club entrance. It is a snazzy place with velvet ropes, red carpets, flashing lights, and masses of wealthy Colombians. Talia is as excited as I am, her boobs bobbing up and down with each step. Pazit is spellbound, like a young kid at Disneyland. I get the feeling she's never been to a club in her life.

Let me just say that I refuse to wait in a line at clubs. Back in high school, Ronit and I were never on any guest lists, so we always had to find creative ways to get in— which frequently involved pretending to be foreigners and speaking in heavy English accents as we brushed past the bouncer. It usually worked. Sure, it would have been nice to be the six-foot-tall, gorgeous models ushered in by some hot guy with a great ass and a tasteful black sweater, but Ronit and I knew that wasn't in the cards for us. We fought back not because we wanted to hang out with the pretty people but because we liked the music and would dance the night away without a care in the world. When you accept that you will never be accepted, you are released from the hunger to be accepted. Put *that* in a fortune cookie.

This time is different, however. *We* are the cool kids. Or at least we're with them. Dozens of hot girls and well-gelled gentlemen rush over to the boys as we arrive, and much cheek kissing and small talk ensue, while the girls and I ogle our surroundings.

We follow the boys to the first velvet rope. Guillermo gives the bouncer a kiss on the cheek, and we all proceed to the second checkpoint, where a stunning Penelope Cruz clone is waiting.

"Stop!" the bouncer barks. We turn around, but Guillermo keeps walking, that verb clearly not in his lexicon. "The girls can't go in with those shoes."

I'm sporting black Pumas, Talia has Tevas on, and Pazit is wearing dirt-encrusted hiking boots.

Guillermo looks around, embarrassed. "Why did you wear those shoes?" Guillermo asks as if our soles were bathed in the blood of Christ.

I'm getting tired of this whole "not good enough to be here" routine.

"We're backpacking, we didn't pack our stilettos!" I fire back. "Let's go, girls. We'll take a cab home!" Talia and Pazit nod, and we bravely descend the stairs in an act of defiance. Guillermo's guilt overpowers his embarrassment at our footwear, and he convinces the bouncer to let us in.

◌

The club is one of those domey, strobey, lose-your-hearing-before-you reach-25 kind of places. The music is a combination of Europop and electronica, which does not seem to register with the Colombian clubbers, who insist on salsa dancing to all the songs, regardless of their genre. You try salsaing to Daft Punk, it ain't easy.

Once on the dance floor, Guillermo and Pedro immediately go scavenging, leaving Talia, Pazit, and me to dance with each other in an odd triangle. Surprisingly, it feels good to be with these girls right now. I like Pazit; she's a good kid. Hairy, but good—no pretense, no attitude, knows who she is, and is cool with it. I could learn a thing or twenty from her.

32

BACK-DOOR POLICY

I can't stop thinking about Idan. His beautiful face has been permanently etched in my brain. (Doesn't mean I'm shallow, just means the fact that he won the gene pool lottery should not be held against him.) I am fully aware that I barely know the guy, that he's unavailable, and that I'm an immature idiot who's still addicted to teen cues of love, but the heart is stronger than the mind, and those who try to conquer the heart with the mind end up being miserable. Or happily married with three kids and a stable job. But I'm not there yet.

I wonder what he's doing right now. Is Chelsea giving him a rectal rub? She's probably good at that. I don't know why I went straight for the anus on that one. Maybe it's all my stomach ailments. There's no arguing that the rectum is a very dominant part of my body. Not size-wise. That would make me a Bonobo, and there would be no hope for me then. But in terms of sheer activity, it's not exactly dormant.

And that's why I refuse to have anal sex. In case you were curious. Of course guys always try to persuade me otherwise, but I see the anus as the portal to the cesspool of hell that is my gastrointestinal system, and I'd like to keep it in that exclusive capacity. Which is exactly what I tell these guys, which instantly kills their desire not only to have anal sex but to get anywhere near the lower regions of my body, and the evening ends with a swift putting on of clothes, a speedy exit, and my butthole intact.

Would I let Idan enter through the back door if he asked? That's a good question. I don't know. I'd give him a finger in, I know that much. Hell, I'd give him a few fingers.

It must be love.

33

BAKSHISH

Sometimes God works in mysterious ways. This week, His heavenly gifts come in the form of an unprecedented offer from Avianca Airlines: three flights to anywhere in Colombia for $99. We all agree our next stop should be Santa Marta, which is the jumping off point for Park Tairona, home to the most beautiful beach in South America. (I will spare you tales of the tiny paper plane that takes us there since we've had our fill of body-function anecdotes.)

Santa Marta is like nothing we've experienced so far. The population is mostly warm, black, and welcoming. The humid air is fragrant, ethereal, and riddled with mosquitoes. It is distinctively and magically Caribbean.

The moomlatz guesthouse here is hoppin'. The massive black woman who runs the place greets us with a smile and a coconut. A bunch of muchilleros sit in the courtyard drinking and chatting, stray cats race playfully around, a ribby dog sits languidly in the corner.

The girls and I spend the evening enjoying the warm summer air, gathering information on Park Tairona, which, adhering to Colombian stereotypes, consists mainly of coca fields. The park entrance is heavily guarded, and there are snipers stationed at random locations throughout the park to protect the fields. Of course, the only people who actually go to the park during this state of emergency are Israelis. Apparently, the real trick, besides reaching the beach without getting shot, is getting into the park in the first place, which involves giving the guards $30 to turn a blind eye and hoping for the best.

It's a tried-and-true technique that no muchillero has encountered any difficulties with, and I suggest we leave first thing in the morning after a good night's sleep and some bikini waxing.

"Thirty bucks is a lot of money," Talia says. If spending a buck for a sock is a stretch, what'd you expect convincing her to spend $30 would be—cake?

"Yeah, I don't think we should pay that kind of money," Pazit chimes in.

Watch it, Pazit. I recently said good things about you, don't ruin it now.

"What else do you propose?" I ask. "It's not like we can just sneak past the guards."

"Yes, we can," Pazit says.

Talia nods, as if they had already discussed this.

"How?" I ask, trying to suppress that uneasy feeling of being the odd man out again.

"We go at night," Pazit replies with confidence. "That way the guards don't see us, and we get in for free."

"That's crazy," I say, "and dangerous!"

"Yeah," Talia says, nodding in agreement. "But it's even crazier paying thirty bucks to get in."

I can't win these ridiculously reasoned arguments. I've had enough. But I don't want to die.

"You know what, how about I pay for you and Pazit?"

"What is that supposed to mean?"

"You don't want to spend the thirty bucks, I don't want to die, so I will spend it for you."

"I don't need your money."

"I know you don't, but I need you to need my money because this is getting ridiculous."

"If you don't want to go with us, then Pazit and I will go at night, and you can just meet us there the next morning."

Oh, shit's gonna be hitting the fan now.

"I can't believe you're pulling that crap on me again, Talia."

"What crap?"

"If I don't do what *you* want, you don't do what *I* want, you just keep doing what *you* want, and tell me to do what *I* want!"

"What??"

"You never compromise. You want to have your cake and eat it too, all the time."

"That's not true."

"Yes, it is!"

"No, it's not!!"

By now everyone at the guesthouse is staring at our little shouting match.

"I thought we were traveling together, Talia, but we're not. We just happen to be in some of the same places at the same time."

"What do you want from me, Iris? You've known me for ten years, you know who I am, why are you suddenly shocked at my behavior?"

"I don't know, I guess I was hoping you would change."

"Why? I don't want to change."

"Well *I* want you to change."

"That's ridiculous."

"I know!"

Talia can't contain a laugh. I can't either. The tension dissipates.

"Does that mean you'll pay the thirty dollars and go with me during daylight hours?"

"No."

"Fine. I'll get my night gear together."

Ↄↄ

Pazit volunteers to organize the essentials for our jungle excursion, which include two weeks' worth of food, water, and supplies. I'm happy we have her on board; this is definitely her specialty. And we'll be using her turbogaz, which is kind of exciting.

Pazit shows up for our departure in her hiking uniform. Come to think of it, she's always in her hiking uniform. The woman never changes clothes. She doesn't smell, but she doesn't change clothes either. Maybe her eyebrows absorb excess odor. My hiking uniform consists of a sundress and flip-flops.

Apparently "essentials" in Pazit's mind are plastic bags full of pots and pans, fourteen packs of pasta, and a canister of salt. So much for a diverse dietary experience oceanside.

We walk down a wide dirt road into the park and reach the guard shack fairly quickly. The light is off but we can hear low chatter inside. We tiptoe past the shack toward the park grounds. Jesus, Pazit's one heavy breather. It's like she has man-lungs. One of my flip-flops curls under at the toe, sending me off balance. The pots clank in the plastic bag. We freeze, waiting for sniper fire.

Nothing.

Whew.

We scurry into the park and walk for another hundred yards or so, reaching a dense jungle of sorts.

"Where's the beach?" I ask.

"It's not for a while," Pazit says.

"What do you mean, 'not for a while'?"

"We have to hike through the jungle first."

"What? How are we supposed to hike through the jungle like this? I'm wearing flip-flops, it's pitch black out here, and this plastic bag handle is about to rip in half."

"We don't have a choice," she says, skipping along the rocks in her moon boots.

"But we can't see anything!" I say.

"I have a flashlight," Talia announces.

"When did you get a flashlight?" I ask.

"Before I left."

"You didn't tell me that."

"Why would I tell you that I bought a flashlight?"

"I don't know. We're traveling together. I'd like to think that we share that kind of crucial information."

"Iris, don't start."

"Okay, okay, just stay close to me."

"Fine."

Talia turns on her secret flashlight. It illuminates the space seven inches in front of her, leaving Pazit and me in complete darkness.

"Crappy flashlight," I mumble.

"It was the only one they had."

"The only one they had on *sale*."

"Excuse me?"

"Nothing. Let's just go."

Ten minutes into our journey it starts to rain. Torrentially. An unexpected development, one might say. Talia and Pazit proceed unhindered, but walking is now ten times harder for me, my flip-flops constantly slipping on the rocks. With every slip, the plastic bags swing, creating a cacophony of clanging metal, rubber on stone, and bilingual cursing.

After what feels like hours fumbling through the jungle, we hear the sound of the ocean. Pazit pushes through one more palm leaf, and, voilà, the beautiful moonlit Caribbean appears before us. All is silent, save for the quiet caress of the ocean and the creaking of hammocks.

A small, well-toned man approaches, the smell of cigarettes and Caribbean patchouli emanating from his person.

"*Hola!*" he says in a sweet yet gruff voice, impressed with our nighttime gumption.

"*Hola!*" we reply and follow him to a shade structure a few feet from the water. In the center of the structure is a palm tree, to which several hammocks are tied. We quietly lay our stuff on the ground and hop in our hammocks for much-needed slumber.

In case you didn't know, hammocks are designed for people with no spines, or at the very least those who have no desire for comfort or logic. The human body simply isn't built for banana-shaped configurations. These Tairona hammocks are especially taut and challenging. I try turning onto my side but am quickly flipped over and flung to the ground. After several additional attempts at channeling Gumby, I resign myself to lying on my back, hands at my sides, chin touching my chest, and let the cool sea breeze waft me to sleep.

❧

Wow. Tairona at sunrise. It is these kinds of mornings that make me appreciate my sense of sight. The water is emerald green, the sand a golden marshmallow white, the palm trees perfectly spaced at standard postcard intervals.

Talia and Pazit are both still pretzeled asleep so I put on my bathing suit and venture out onto the beach for a walk.

MacGruff is out and about, brandishing a two-foot machete. He spots me and heads my way. Hope he's not in a bad mood.

"*Hola!*" he says again in his sweet, gruff voice.

"*Hola!*" I reply. I could live an entire lifetime with this limited vocabulary and be perfectly content. Life would be a constant meet-and-greet with no need for any meaningful follow-up or inevitable neuroses and dysfunction. I would start the *Hola!* cult, where members would be forbidden to speak anything other than the holy word of *Hola!* Married couples would copulate and after climaxing look at each other and say, "*Hola!*" and all would be well. There would be no substance-filled talk about desires or inadequacies. Children wouldn't be able to complain or whine. They would just greet their parents "*Hola!*" in the morning and "*Hola!*" at night. First dates would never be awkward. They'd be as efficient and as exciting as the ninth date, since everything would feel new and nostalgic at the same time, like in that movie *Groundhog Day*.

MacGruff climbs up a nearby palm tree with amazing alacrity, as if the tree were horizontal and he were on a moving platform.[23] He yells from up top, motioning for me to move out of the way. With a *thwat-thwat* he slices three coconuts off the tree, and with a *bam-bam-bam* they land a few feet away from me with a sandy thud. He then slides down the tree without a hitch. Either the man has no genitalia, or his bloody balls are weeping right now. He slices open a coconut for me, and I

---

23 Do you think airport moving walkways are ridiculous and built for lazy/stupid people only? Do you make a point of not taking the walkways? Do you secretly race the people on the walkway, moving as fast as you can, dragging your carry-on awkwardly behind you, just to beat them to the other side? And when you do, is the satisfaction and superiority you feel over these lazy stupid walkway people priceless? If so, welcome.

drink. I discover that raw coconut milk is sorta tasty and sorta like suntan lotion that has dripped off someone's lower back.

Talia and Pazit appear on the beach, skipping my way excitedly. As expected, Talia's bikini triangles barely cover her nipples. Also as expected, Pazit is not a fan of hair removal. Unfortunate, considering she's Middle Eastern. At least she doesn't dye it blonde like some Persian women do. Those Persian "blondes" are so hairy they have to bleach their body hair to match. They end up looking like a cross between Salma Hayek and Big Bird.

The day is magnificently catatonic. We bake in the sun, and I turn a sexy shade of bronze much faster than normal, miraculously skipping the roasted piglet phase I usually have to endure before attaining a happy golden hue.

Lunchtime arrives, and we bust out the pots and pans. Pazit is no iron chef, and it takes her an hour to get the turbogaz going. A flash rainstorm hits just as the burner lights. Strong winds and flying sand quickly extinguish the flame (so much for bonus features), and we are forced to wait another hour for the rain to stop. Mind you, I haven't had anything but coconut milk since sunrise.

We all sit glumly around the pot waiting for the water to boil, which is not destined to happen anytime soon. I notice MacGruff watching us, perplexed.

I go over to him. "*Hola!*" I say, and then proceed to ask what's up: "*Hola?*"

"*Hola!*" he replies and motions for me to follow him.

Behind a small expanse of palm trees sits a fully functioning, well-lit, little restaurant. With cutlery and everything.

"*Hola!!*" I say, giving him a big hug.

I run back to tell Pazit and Talia the good news.

Pazit looks heartbroken. "I'm still going to cook," she says defiantly. "We shouldn't waste the food."

"What food?" I reply. "We bought fourteen packets of pasta and a packet of salt."

"I'd rather cook. Self-cooked meals always taste better."

She's got to be kidding.

Once again, Talia agrees. "I don't want to spend money if we don't have to."

This time I don't argue or make snide monetary comments. But I don't cave in either.

"Okay, I'll be back for dessert."

They don't grasp the sarcasm in my statement, but they also don't seem to care. At this point neither do I.

სა

Back at the diner, MacGruff brings over an oil lamp and cleans the rusty wood table with his palm. He motions for me to wait and disappears into the kitchen. There is no menu, which is fine. I'm just happy not spending my vacation waiting for water to boil.

He returns a few minutes later with the house (and only) specialty: a large bowl of pasta topped with a blob of ketchup and a large mountain of French fries. Enough starch to petrify a small animal, but I don't care. The meal is culinary bliss—the fries magnificent in their undercooked sogginess, the ketchup as tasty as Santina's bolognese, the copious bed of oil at the bottom a warm and welcome ending to a fantastic meal.

I thank MacGruff for his wizardry and return to see how Talia and Pazit are faring. They have finished eating and are scrubbing the pots and pans with sand and sea water. It starts to pour again. We race back to the structure and cocoon ourselves in our hammocks, swaying to and fro like little Jew-pods fighting the elements.

Night falls. Pazit and Talia fall asleep instantly, but I stay up, finding comfort watching the stormy chaos unfold: trees thrashing, hammocks swaying, waves slamming onto the beach, as if my inner tumult were being released at nature's expense. The post-storm calm is all the more profound and visceral and it sends me into a deep slumber, the kind that follows nineteen hours of crazy sex combined with a kickboxing session and Two-Thai back rub.

I am awakened in the middle of the night by the sound of MacGruff leading a man toward our hammock haven. No doubt another cheapo trying to save a few bucks by sneaking in under cover of darkness. MacGruff leads him to the hammock next to mine. Mystery man pats MacGruff on the back, whispering something in his ear. I can't believe Gruffkie would lead a strange man into our estrogen unit. What if he's some skeezy slimeball who has come to Tairona just to bone unsuspecting hammockers?

The man creeps into his hammock, trying to be as quiet as possible. Stealthy bastard. He lies there for a moment then lets out a relaxed sigh. I realize I've been holding my breath and exhale as well. He knows I'm awake.

"Want a cigarette?" he whispers.

"No thanks," I reply. I can't wait to see Talia's reaction tomorrow morning when she discovers a strange smoker is our new hut mate. She's gonna eat his balls for breakfast.

He strikes a match, and brings it up to the cigarette hanging from his puffy black-man lips.

My heart stops.

"Idan?"

"Iris!" He breaks into his magical smile.

The storm begins again.

34

BOOB BAKE

Idan and I spend the next two hours whispering to each other about everything from Idan's whore days of yore to my traumas at Brown. I avoid asking about Chelsea. I'm sure she'll arrive any minute now. She probably got hung up giving the park guards a back rub. I must say I feel more comfortable talking to Idan than I ever did to egghead Kaufman. Maybe therapists need to be more fucked up themselves, or at least let you know how fucked up they really are. That way you won't feel so pathetic revealing the really messed up shit in your own life.

Idan isn't as baggage-ridden as I am, but he does have a respectable Samsonite collection, and he reveals secrets to me that he has never told anyone. He tells me he's scared of starting university, that his brother is in a juvenile facility, that he contemplated suicide a year ago, that he really doesn't consider Rooli and Laffi to be as close to him as they assume they are.

I tell him that I came on this trip out of a need to escape my depression, that my therapist almost drove me to suicide, and that I'm a better friend to Talia than she is to me. I begin to cry. Jesus. I barely know this guy, and he's already seen me cry twice. He must think I'm made of pussymush. But wait. His eyes have welled up too! We are both made of pussymush! God, this is such a beautiful moment!

He kisses me. His pillow lips are heavenly. His tongue, however, is disproportionately thick and big, and he kisses with an aggressive delivery and high saliva quotient. But I can live with that. Maybe that's a sign of my growth. The old me would have nixed any chance with Idan because of something silly like a saliva quotient, but the new me is enamored by our communication, our connection, and is willing to work with him on his snoggery skills.

When I realize we've reached the point where a paper towel is in order, I pull away, wipe my mouth, and ask the dreaded question. "Where's Chelsea?"

"She's gone back to Australia."

"Oh." (YAY!!) "Why?"

"She's a wonderful woman, but it was a travel fling, nothing more."

"Amazing hands."

"Yes, truly amazing. But no sex drive."

"Really?"

"Yes. She said that part of her was tranquil. I just thought she was frigid."

"So you didn't have sex?"

"Not really. I mean, sure, we had sex, but not as much as I wanted."

"Right."

"How about you? Any travel flings on this trip?"

"Not really."

"Why not?"

"I haven't met anyone I really like. I did kind of hook up with some guy Raoul in Cuzco, but that didn't work out."

"Handsome Raoul?"

"Yes."

"Is he as good as they say?"

"We didn't have sex."

"You didn't? Why not?"

"Conditions weren't right."

"Are you insane?"

"Hah, no. Just a woman with an ill-timed menstrual cycle."

❧

Idan ends up sleeping in my hammock with me. His added weight allows me to shift onto my side, and we manage a nice spooning position that remains stable for the entire night. The sun rises, and I awaken, content yet anxious. Hey, it's a long road from mess to Zen—this is a necessary transitional phase. Idan is sleeping soundly. I know he's going to wake up and think, *What the hell am I doing next to this woman? What was I thinking? Must have been the sea breeze going to my head*, so I lie there, frozen, cherishing every second that our bodies are in contact before the magic ends and my hammock becomes unstable again.

I spend the next petrified hour mentally playing out the various scenarios of how Idan would leave. Talia opens her eyes and sees Idan beside me. Something in her eyes tells me she's happy for me. That's one perk of having an indifferent friend: She may not care, but she doesn't get jealous either. And when she's happy for you, she's really happy for you. Well, as happy as an indifferent person can be.

Idan finally wakes and sees me deep in thought. "What are you thinking about?"

I could lie and make up something trite and charming. But I'm not going to, not with Idan. The truth spills out of me, in white-water fashion. "I'm wondering at what point you're going to freak out and leave me."

"Why would you think that?" he says, not as surprised as I expected/hoped.

My verbal river continues to smash up against the rocks. "I don't know. Maybe I'm trying to prepare myself for pain by obsessing over it, getting used to the idea or something, but I know that never works. I've obsessed over my parents' death for as long as I can remember. Playing the scenario over and over again—how it would suddenly be just me and my brother, who would freak out because suddenly my father wouldn't be there to visit him every week and where would I be? Would I visit him every week? The one time I visited him alone because my father was out of town he hit himself over and over again screaming, 'Where's

Aba? Where's Aba?' over and over and over again. I cried so hard I couldn't stop. It was so bad, I was hysterical. I kept crying the entire drive back to Manhattan, and that only reinforced my terror of what would happen one day when my parents are both gone. So I fooled myself into thinking if you visualize it enough, if you actually imagine the pain that you will feel once that tragedy happens, then when it happens you'll be better prepared."

I check to see Idan hasn't fallen asleep yet. On the contrary—he is, in fact, completely engaged. I want to stop rambling but I can't, the words just keep spilling out with the pain.

"One night I was sitting in my apartment in Tel Aviv, and I suddenly imagined that I would get a phone call in the middle of the night from a hospital in New York informing me that my father had come down with a mysterious illness and they were not sure he was going to make it. The vision was so disturbing that I got angry at myself for envisioning it. How fucked up am I? I'm too young to have this kind of warped shit in my brain. And then two days later, at three in the morning, I got a phone call. From a hospital in New York. My father had come down with a mysterious illness. They weren't sure he was going to make it, and I needed to get to New York as soon as humanly possible. I couldn't breathe. I ran to the bathroom and lost five pounds. I mean, why did I have to be clairvoyant for something horrible? Why couldn't I have seen a vision that involved me and a well-bathed Johnny Depp engaging in festive coitus?"

Idan laughs, squeezing my hand. "What happened then?"

"I flew to New York that night to stay with my Dad's wife at their house in the Bronx and spent the next couple of weeks in a state of constant breakdown. My father was in the intensive care unit—unconscious, puffy, bloated from water retention, his lungs full of fluid. The worst part is, they didn't know what was wrong with him. Every minute might be his last, they kept telling me. I lost fifteen more pounds during those two weeks, a walking skeleton clacking back and forth from the waiting room to the ICU where I bugged the doctors and nurses for updates every ten minutes. I couldn't eat, couldn't sleep, constantly terrified I would get the horrible news at any moment. So what good did all that mental/emotional prep do me? Nothing. No good at all. When things were good, I was worried they'd turn horrible. When they were horrible, they still felt horrible.

"So I turned to God. My belief had always been present, sometimes stronger, sometimes more distant, but it was never a practical belief—I never sought solace in God. I always thought, *Yeah, there's a God*, but that's about it. It felt weird asking God for anything. I mean, what did He owe me? It's not like He was serving a purpose or I was serving a purpose. He was just present, kind of like mediocre jazz at a bar, only celestial, transcendent, and almighty.

"But that night I prayed. I closed my eyes and for the first time in my life I felt what it meant to pray for something. My entire being, crying and begging God to make my dad better. I realized I had to offer something in return. I mean, even God doesn't want to feel like he's getting fucked over. So

I told God if He made my father better I would quit eating shellfish. You have to understand, I *loved* shellfish. Give me a bucket of oysters, mussels, escargot, shrimp cocktail, I'm in heaven. So this was no little promise, no small commitment."

"I love shrimp!" Idan exclaims.

"So you understand the level of sacrifice I'm talking here."

"Absolutely. Go on."

"Anyway God realized it too. Because the next day they figured out what was wrong with my father. Some archaic pneumonia called Legionnaires' Disease. Within a week of treatment he was breathing and conscious and happy to be alive. Happy enough that he got pissed at me for using his cell phone so much to call my mom during the ordeal. But we won't get into that."

Idan caresses my cheek gently.

"I love that you told me all that," he says, pulling me closer.

"You do? Those are twenty minutes of your life you're never going to get back."

He chuckles. "I've got all the time in the world for you," he says.

There is love in his eyes.

ᴄ⳽

We spend the next few days kissing a lot and spooning in the hammock. I know he wants sex—not because I'm assuming all men want sex but because he states that he wants to have sex with me. Several times. An hour. But I'm scared. I'm scared I won't be good enough for him, that he'll get bored, that the sex will be slobby and ruin the beauty of what we have. So I tell him I'm too shy to have sex on the beach, that we have no privacy, that I don't want a stray ant crawling up my poon.

God, I'm lame. Why do I have to get all weird and celibate now? Here's the love of my life, and I pull a line about poon ants? I mean, come on! As understanding as he is, or pretending to be, it won't last forever.

I better deliver soon or risk losing him.

35

SKI BUNNY

I wake up this morning to find Idan isn't lying beside me. That's it, he's gone. I knew he would leave.

No, he's actually just walking around the restaurant for some reason. Thank God.

"Idan!" I call out, waving maniacally.

He smiles and walks back, an intense, determined look in his eyes that I've never seen before.

"Good morning," I say, somewhat nervously.

"I want to get some cocaine," he says, as if asking me to pass the nondairy creamer.

"What?" (Cocaine is the drug of angry hedge-fund assholes, not my lovely, kind Idan). "Why do you want cocaine?"

"Why not?"

Fair enough. The only possible response to that will make me sound like a concerned parent, so I pretend not to have a good answer, even though the list in my head is a foot long.

"Have you done it before?" I ask.

"Yeah, a bunch of times in Ecuador, but this is obviously the place to get it. It's supposed to be super pure and super cheap."

"Isn't it dangerous to start looking for cocaine now?"

"I'm sure the owner has some. I just can't find him."

Oh no. What will MacGruff think of his sweet coconut girl now? How will he respond with his limited *Hola!* vocabulary to a request for life-endangering substances? The chances for miscommunication are endless. He may think Idan is DEA and alert the actual Cocanistas, and they'll come and chop our heads off and drink our head juice. I pray that he has gone back to town to buy ketchup and grease and won't be back for a week, but a moment later we both hear the festive *Hola!* call and Idan rushes over and takes him aside to discuss business, gesticulating a joyful sniffing motion. MacGruff nods in immediate comprehension and pats Idan on the back.

Idan's enthusiasm for cocaine is disconcerting, but I fight the urge to start a flaw list like I usually do. After all, I'm the uptight one. Everyone does cocaine, and if you're in Colombia and you don't do it then you're just stupid.

MacGruff returns with a *huge* baggie full of coke. Idan hands him a tiny wad of cash, his eyes glistening with excitement as he dips his finger in the bag. I am suddenly invisible.

"Are you okay?" he asks.

Oh wait, not that invisible. "Yes."

"Do you want any?"

"No."

"Why not?"

"I just don't."

"Okay."

He rubs some on his gums and then snorts some.

"Wow. This shit is good. Do you know how much I paid for this?"

"No idea." Wish I knew what the going rate was.

"This would cost five hundred dollars back in Israel. I paid twenty."

Talia would be proud.

Idan puts on some trance music and starts dancing. He looks possessed—pounding the ground, his pupils large enough to contain a small Ukrainian village. I just stare, part of me wanting to be part of this apparently exciting experience, the other part wondering why on earth people like cocaine. Which is not to say I've had no experience with the drug. Albeit not physically.

❧

Month three at Brown: post Carlos and Koo Yim, pre-Brodie and shit village. I was busy making friends with the urban hipster set. My new best friend, Vincent, a tall, muscular man of mixed ethnicity, took me to his friend's house on Barnes Street for a little gathering.

A man with oily blonde hair, a puffy face, and beady blue eyes opened the door. Through a cloud of pot smoke, I could see a large living room where various other mixed ethnics were lounging on used couches and leather recliners.

"Brian, my man!" Vincent said, launching into a combo ghetto-bro hug that involved shoulder grazing and back patting.

"Hi! I'm Iris!" I said, rushing over to engage in a ghetto-bro hug too, the smaller, less coordinated version.

"How's it going?" Brian replied, cool and inattentive.

"Great! I'm doing great! First year back in America, and I feel grand!" I said, desperately wanting to be liked by this odd-looking creature.

Beady Brian looked at me, took a hit of his joint, and pulled Vincent aside.

I remained standing outside the door, confused. Vincent returned, concerned.

"We should go," Vincent said.

"What's wrong?" I asked.

"Brian thinks you're too coked up to be at the party. You kinda freaked him out."

"Too coked up? What is he talking about?" I cried, truly shocked. "I've never touched cocaine in my life. This is just me being me!"

"You mean you're amped up like this all the time?"

"Yes!"

Vincent looked at me, clearly not believing anyone could be this amped up all the time. "Look, Brian is one of the biggest coke dealers on campus, so he knows his shit. You might want to take care of yourself if you have a problem."

"But I don't have a prob—"

"Seriously dude, denial is the first obstacle, you need to take care of that shit. Coke can ruin your life."

Well, he was right about that part. Cocaine is changing Idan right before my eyes and it's scary. Forget the sweaty mess and robotic foot pounding. What's really upsetting is that his usually sweet smile has turned aggressive—and stays aggressive for the next few hours. Nevertheless, I watch him lovingly, like a mother waiting for her A.D.D. child to tire of the sandbox.

His pounding foot has managed to dig a hole halfway to the Orient. I'm waiting for the paddy-hatted squinting Chinaman to pop up and shove a bowl of rice in his face while the Looney Tunes music takes us to the end credits.

Idan suddenly looks worried.

"You step on a Chinaman?" I ask.

He just stares at me. Tough crowd.

Shit. He looks horrible.

"Are you all right?"

"My heart."

"What about it?"

"It's beating really hard."

"Maybe you should stop pounding the ground."

"No, no, I don't want to do that." He pounds faster.

"Idan, you're scaring me. Please sit down."

"I'm fine I'm fine I'm fine. I'll be fine."

"Here." I hand him some water.

He drinks.

"Idan, please stop dancing. You should let your heart rest."

"You're beautiful."

Whoa. That came out of nowhere. "What did you say?"

"I said you're beautiful. Very, very beautiful."

Nobody has ever said that to me. Men have told me I'm quirky and cute and adorable and feisty and all those other elfin qualities, but never beautiful. You could claim it's not Idan but the cocaine talking. That would imply that I don't believe I'm beautiful. To be honest, I didn't believe it. Until now. I feel beautiful. I am. I *am* beautiful, goddammit. I am a beautiful woman taking care of her coke fiend boyfriend. And I love him for it.

Am I still afraid this movie-love is going to end in ninety minutes once the popcorn has reached its nausea-inducing phase of the viewing experience? Absolutely. But I don't flee. Intsead I let Idan fall asleep in my arms, all sweaty and stinky, white residue encrusted on his nostrils. MacGruff comes by and examines the crater near our hammocks.

"*Buena cocaina, ha?*" he asks, as if he were the one who harvested the coca leaves. Wait a minute . . .

಄

The next few days and nights meld into one another in a surreal fashion. Idan has accepted that we will not have sex at the park, and I have gotten over my fear of him leaving me for another sex partner. You know why? There are no other women here! No hot Danish chicks with tan skin and blue eyes, no sluts in fleece, nobody. Besides Talia and Pazit, I'm it.

Well, at least I thought so. Until Talia walks over with some surprising news.

"Helena Christensen has just arrived and is eating fries with her legs open!"

"What??"

"Just kidding. Pazit and I are heading to Cartagena."

I find this substantially more disturbing.

"What do you mean you and Pazit are heading to Cartagena?"

"I'll give you girls some privacy," Idan says, walking off, bless his tactful heart.

"You're obviously with Idan now, and Pazit and I have gotten really bored. So we're going to Cartagena."

"But I don't want to part ways with you now."

I can feel the separation anxiety/abandonment complex coming back with a vengeance.

"I'm not angry, Iris. It's okay."

"No, really, I don't want you to go."

I thought finding the love of my life would alleviate me of this syndrome but it clearly has not. Maybe because friends have always been more important to me than men, maybe because I believe men are unreliable, that relationships are fleeting, that friendship should always be the priority. In high school, I always put my girlfriends first and was always disappointed when they put their boyfriends first. Isn't it time I put the man in my life in first position? Especially since I'm getting my girlfriend's approval? Shit, what do I do?

I finally ask Talia the question that's been on my mind forever.

"Do you want to travel with Pazit . . . without me?"

"I don't care either way. Whatever you want to do is fine with me."

I know, I know, Talia will never give me the answer that I want and I should stop trying.

"Do whatever makes you happy, Iris," she continues. "You really seem to like this guy."

"We just met."

"So?"

"I want to come with you."

"You sure?"

"Yes, but . . . "

"But what?"

"I want him to come too."

"Sure, whatever."

&

Idan is thrilled that I've invited him to join us. He admits to watching my conversation with Talia from afar and reveals that he was worried I was going to leave. So nice to have someone else use the word "worried" for a change. He's also probably psyched to have access to more sex-friendly surfaces before his dick falls off from inactivity.

36

STARING AT THE CEILING

Cartagena is all gorgeous European architecture, good food, and music in the streets. The moomlatz guesthouse is a beautiful old building with arched windows and elaborate tile floors.

The owner asks for our passports. Talia and Pazit fork theirs over. Idan pulls me aside.

"I have a surprise for you."

"What?"

"We're going to a nice hotel for the night! It's five stars!"

Fuck. Poor guy. I know he can't afford a five-star hotel. He must really be horny. I could try to pull the whole "forget checking in, let's go sightseeing!" and then feign post-sightseeing exhaustion, but I can't. I have to take the plunge here and do the deed. Time to give the panickino in my gut a big doobie and tell it to calm the fuck down.[24]

---

24 Panickino, *n.* Microscopic creature whose only purpose is to induce anxiety in its host. [Latin/Old Italian: small panic.]

❧

The second we enter the hotel room, Idan attacks me, full slobber ahead. I take a breath, making a conscious decision to go for it. I slobber back, and we toss each other to and fro like two underweight whales. Before I know it, our clothes are completely off, and Idan is pulling my poon onto his face. He is an enthusiastic cunnilinguist, but his big tongue isn't as focused and pointed as I wish it were. It has more of a paint-roller effect on my vagina, which is fun for the first few seconds but quickly numbs the whole area. Once he really gets going, all I can think about is that urban myth about that girl who put dog food between her legs so her dog would eat her out, not knowing all her friends were hiding in the room waiting to surprise her for her birthday. Maybe she could teach me how to enjoy this lapping technique.

On a positive note, his member is healthy, lengthy, and girthy. Eager to get the deed done, I wrap it in latex and stick it in with almost no sensuality or technique. We have sex, the whole time my mind racing and repeating the mantra *Stop thinking, just go with it, stop thinking, go with it!* which of course results in being anything but present. Which could be a good thing because, before I can judge the act and freak out about the experience, it's over. Idan lasted as long as he could, and he did an admirable job considering what he's been through the last few weeks.

As far as I'm concerned, by committing the act itself, Idan and I crossed a mile-high emotional hurdle, even though it didn't involve the same vulnerability, tenderness, or intimacy that we had when gazing into each other's eyes or caressing each other's hands.

He's clearly disappointed by the experience. Maybe it's because I made no eye contact the entire time, or when I told him kindly that slobbering on my poon leads to numbness fairly quickly and could he try and be a bit more focused with the tongue action, or the fact that I told him to *"Come now!"* numerous times while not displaying any signs of orgasm on my end. Then again maybe I'm wrong and he thought the sex was great; God knows men have lower standards in that department.

Any foreplay last night, Jack?

Nah! Who needs it, Pete? A hard-on and open portal is always good enough for me!

I hear that, brother!

I kiss Idan softly on the lips. He looks at me, a measure of pain in his eyes. I want to apologize for being so fucked up, but I fight the urge and nestle in his armpit. Hopefully he'll be patient.

∞

We reunite with Talia at the guesthouse the next morning.

"I missed you!" she says. Wow, second time in three weeks, I can't believe my ears. "How was it?"

"Great!" I lie.

"Cool!"

"Where's Pazit?"

"Her turbogaz broke. She went to find a service provider."

"Good thinking."

"Your beds are ready by the way. We pushed two single ones together for you guys."

"Actually, Idan and I are gonna take our own room tonight if that's cool," I say, shocked at my ability to communicate in a clear and concise fashion.

Idan looks at me, over the moon.

I'm gonna make this work, goddammit. I don't care how much slobbering is involved, Poonie and I will just have to deal.

37

THE STINKING ROSE

The next few days in Cartagena are scorchingly hot. Too hot to leave the room, too hot to breathe. To top it all off, my stomach has decided to take in a new tenant, this time of the amoebic kind, the symptoms of which I will not detail. Let's just say Idan's lack of utter disgust is a true sign of his knighthood. He wants to take me to the hospital, but I refuse, recounting my last experience with the Braveheart-Kojakian school of medicine. So I partake in the holistic remedy for amoebas: garlic. Huge, raw, unadulterated cloves of garlic swallowed whole.

Idan is skeptical that any human can swallow raw cloves that size. But I prove him wrong. Maybe it's God's way of telling me I need to pursue a career in drug smuggling. Iris Bahr: Master Mule Cocaine-filled Condom Swallower. I can see it now: MacGruff and I will start a cartel, the feared Bahr Cartel, which will take over the Medellín-Miami circuit. The locals will fear us. The DEA will hate us. Assholes on Wall Street will worship us. Beady Brian will tell his friends "I knew her when . . . " I will be Idan's main provider, and he will start his own business providing backyard hole-digging services, and we will live happily ever after.

I return from the bathroom a garlickey mess, only to find a sweaty Idan splayed on the bed, butt naked.

"You smell like an Italian restaurant," he says.

"Sorry about that."

"No, it smells good. God, I'm hungry."

"Me too."

"Let me eat you out."

Oh boy. The man is a saint, but I have absolutely no desire to get lapped up at the moment. But he's already down there flapping his tongue silly.

You know what, it's time he got pleasured too.

Here's a shocker: I've never given a blow job. Ever. I tried once, but the guy smelled like peanuts down there, and I couldn't go through with it. It's not right to receive pleasure without reciprocating. Not that Idan's oral fiesta is that pleasurable, but the poor guy is making the effort, and it's not like I can file his tongue down to my desired specifications or anything. I want to make him feel good, but I'm more scared of failing him in this way than I am with the mechanical sex.

"Idan?"

He gives a final lap of the tongue. I can't feel a damn thing; he might as well be playing Sudoku down there. "Yes?"

"I want to give you a blow job."

"Okay."

I decide to take the honest route again. "I don't really know how. I've never really done it before."

"Really? Do you not like it? Because if you don't like it, I don't want you to do it."

(Lie! Any man who tells you that is lying!)

"No, I'm sure I'll like it. I mean, I'm not sure, but I'm willing to try. Guide me."

"Okay."

I descend toward the target nervously. I can feel Idan get excited. I sniff around . . . no peanut odor, so that's good. The entire room still smells like a Trattoria. I put his shlong in my mouth. It's bigger than I thought and stretches my mouth to full capacity. Mind you, I have a small mouth. As a child, I had to have numerous teeth removed by a very mean dentist who had the gentleness of the Butcher of Lyon. Only he was Jewish. And not a Nazi. The point is, I am aware that this tiny mouth is a perk for Idan but a downside for my jaw.

I also realize I can't just stay static like this and have to proceed to the next step.

I put his member as far down my mouth as it will go, which isn't far. I go up and down for a few cycles. I try to accept a little more each time. If I lift the roof of my mouth, somehow the angle allows his member to enter my throat area, which I've heard is a good thing. Idan's eyes are closed. I can't tell if he's enjoying this or dreaming of better pastures that involve a woman with skills. I run a few more cycles in this fashion, hoping my gag reflex doesn't kick in. So far so good.

"No teeth," he says.

I stop, not knowing how to proceed. I mean, I have teeth in my mouth. How am I supposed to get rid of them? I put my hands on the base of his penis to gain further depth into my throat and manage to lessen the tooth contact. I'm a bit dizzy, maybe because there is no oxygen coming into my lungs. Must breathe through nose. I manage to do so with surprising skill, circulating the air calmly and fluidly, not missing a beat of penis time. I've now got him in almost entirely. Up and down I go, stimulating, toothlessly sucking and nose-breathing with amazing grace, skill, and appropriate force. I even manage a few testicle rubs.

"Oh my God, Iris! You are amazing."

Damn right, I am! I wish I had a penis right now, this looks unbelievable!

I feel some internal bubbling. I think he's about to come. I want to swallow it.

(Lie! Any woman who tells you that is lying!)

But I'm not quite ready for that yet. So I wrap things up with a few hand jerks, and he comes all over himself, a huge smile on his face.

His bliss is interrupted by a knock at the door.

"Iris, it's Talia."

I cover Idan with a towel and open the door. Talia crinkles her nose.

"It smells like an Italian brothel in here."

Idan releases an amused snort.

"Bingo!"

"Pazit's leaving for Venezuela tomorrow. I thought we'd buy her a refill cartridge for her turbogaz as a going away gift."

"Great idea!"

"Oh and I reconfirmed our flights. We're all set for tomorrow."

"What?" I ask, looking back at Idan, shocked. How could I forget—Talia and I are scheduled to return to Quito tomorrow, where she'll catch a flight back to Tel Aviv and I'll head back to Providence to start my sophomore year in hell.

Idan sits up abruptly. Talia catches a quick glimpse of testicle and looks away.

"You leave tomorrow?" he asks, fear in his voice.

It dawns on me that we never really thought about the future—that he's going back to Israel to start university, that I am going back to Brown, and that neither of these things is going to change.

"Yes." A flash flood of sadness washes over me, destroying the Happy and Content beachfront guesthouses I had only recently erected.

Talia heads back to her room. Idan's eyes well up. I didn't realize he was that into me. I didn't think it was possible. My mind races through all the men whose hearts I've broken, and it dawns on me that at the time I didn't believe they were broken, which is why I kept repeating my detrimental patterns. Instead, I kept finding reasons that these men were upset or hurt: It was a bruised ego, nothing to do with me. They didn't really love me, they loved the "idea" of me. They had no clue what was really inside me. And most importantly, they would find a new girl to replace me in a day or two, a girl they would really fall in love with, a normal girl.

But for the first time in my life I look at Idan and I believe him. I believe that I am truly loved, all of me: the good, the bad, the neurotic, the scared, the funny, the crazy. And it scares the hell out of me, and it makes me cry so hard for all the love lost and all my stupidity and fear and the pain I've caused and the pain I've experienced that I fill the bed with garlicky tears. Tears that Idan kisses lovingly off my face.

We sit there for a moment, shifting to technical details to forget the pain.

"I'm supposed to meet Rooli and Laffi in San José for a few days before we fly back to Tel Aviv."

"Oh."

"Iris." Idan squeezes my hand.

"Yes?"

"Do you want me to come with you to New York?"

The answer comes immediately. "Yes."

I hold in a garlic burp with all my might and we hug, the mutual relief overwhelming.

∾

Are we just postponing our inevitable goodbye? It's not like Idan is about to move to Providence. I mean, what would he do there—join a frat on a guest-member basis? He's going to come to New York, we're going to spend three days together agonizing over our real goodbye, and then we will experience the same agony again. But we have no choice. We are in love. Hence we are masochistic, addicted, and stupid. I couldn't be happier. After all, life is just a sequence of events before the inevitable final goodbye anyway, and all we can do is make these events as pleasant as possible, even if they don't have a point.

Right?

38

CUTLERY CONFESSIONS

It feels weird to be alone with Talia again. Something has shifted or died, but I can't tell what. Talia does care about me, but she cares about herself more, and if we stopped being friends tomorrow she wouldn't lose any sleep over it. But I knew that already. I guess what has changed is that it doesn't hurt anymore. Not because I care about Talia less, but because I know now there are people out there who *would* lose sleep over it. Like Idan. And some other friends I haven't found yet. The point is, they are out there, and I deserve to have them in my life.

Was Talia a good travel partner? Sure, she was low maintenance, low drama, relaxed, supportive. And most important, she wasn't critical of me. Which helped me be less critical of me. Her indifference to me and the complexities of my personality made *me* a bit more indifferent to my complexities. (Yes, they're no longer issues or baggage— they're "complexities.")

Once in Quito, we head back to the same guesthouse I almost died in. As a celebration of my survival, the owner upgrades us to her largest room on the top floor. She's not kidding. The room is actually five adjacent rooms with a queen size bed in each. Talia and I leap around the beds like little kids, as if we scored the presidential suite at the Waldorf-Astoria.

Within less than a day, however, our suite fills up to capacity with seven Israeli men en route to Colombia. They are a rowdy bunch, and for the next few days we and our newly formed gang smokes an exorbitant amount of pot, roams the streets, and buys quirky clothing straight out of the Court of the Crimson King. I naturally become the entertainer of the group, enacting hour-long improvised skits for my stoned audience that encompass a wide variety of scenarios from South Central gangstas to Colonial Williamsburg. They prove to be an easy crowd on the humor side but challenging on the attention one.

I wonder what Idan is doing with his buddies right now. Is he cheating on me? Fuck. Why would I even think that? Why would my mind go there? I'm the one who's cavorting around with seven men, one of whom spoons me at night. Is that wrong? Am I just protecting myself by crossing the inappropriate line so as to be less hurt if he does? That's a ridiculous way of thinking. And is spooning cheating? I certainly wouldn't want Idan spooning some chick right now.

Anything I feel a need to hide should not be happening, including the spooning. But I won't tell Idan because I don't want to hurt him. Okay, that's bullshit—I won't tell him because I'm scared of his reaction. Best to stop the spooning. And maybe ease off the pot. My mind is going a lethargic mile a minute, the worst possible combination.

I decide to leave a day early and surprise Idan at the San José airport since I know what flight he's booked on to New York.

I give Talia a truly loving unconditional hug (yep, I found it!!) and a warm kiss goodbye. I don't know when and if our paths will cross again, but I do know this: My days of desperate giving are over. I will wait for her to contact me, and if she doesn't, that's okay too. I will love her just the same.

૮૭

I get to Idan's departure gate about an hour early. My heart pounds as I scan the crowd waiting for him to arrive. Maybe he'll have another girl on his arm and tell me, "I'm sorry Iris, I met this girl, Vera, two days ago, we spooned, and I realized I wasn't in love with you anymore."

God, my mind is a sad, angry little casino.[25]

I suddenly see Laffi and Rooli trudging their way to the gate. No Idan. Oh wait, there he is, tying his shoe. I leap out of my seat, launching several feet into the air. The entire terminal notices, Idan included. His face lights up like a Chanukah bush. He runs my way. My heart soars. He picks me up and gives me the best plump-lip kiss ever. I look away, ashamed.

---

25 I credit my dear friend Patrick for this phrase, only he was referring to Harrah's in Atlantic City.

"What's wrong?" he asks.

"I spooned some guy in Quito."

He laughs and kisses me again. "That's okay. It doesn't matter."

Shit. "Does that mean you spooned somebody too?"

"No, of course not. I'm just happy to see you."

I hug him hard enough to unplug the slot machines for a brief moment.

39

CARDIAC COERCION

We land in New York at night and head to Idan's friend Shlomi's place. Shlomi has been lovingly nicknamed Snake. I do not like Snake. He keeps staring at my arm hair. Mind you, I do NOT have a lot of arm hair. I've seen girls with a lot of arm hair, and I am not one of them. But I'm not a hairless Asian either and prefer to not be reminded of that fact. My arms are also really thin. Not spindly, but thin enough to be nicknamed Holocaust Survivor by Yoni, the cute surfer dude in high school who pretended to like me so I would help him with his English homework.

Snake lives in a tiny shithole fifth-floor walk-up in the East Village. He does lots of coke and works in the moving business. This is par for the course for many Israelis, either before or after their big army trip: get a job at a moving company, live in a tiny shithole apartment, go clubbing every night, and "live the dream." Luckily Idan has opted to go coke-free since the Chinaman episode.

I have to go back to Brown tomorrow. I can't believe it. It's almost like I'd never been there, like the *Big Fat Blue Guide* is still sitting on my bed and I can choose to put it back on the shelf and decide to study in Israel instead. Is that what I want? I don't know. I'm very confused right now. Well, maybe not confused, just—

God, I'm confused about being confused. This is bad. I'm not excited about going back, I'm definitely not excited about leaving Idan, but I'm not eager to stay either. I'm just . . . sad.

"What are you thinking about?" Idan asks.

God, he can read me well. You forget how lucky you are until you date a putz who only gets that something is wrong when you're sobbing and bleeding from your eyeballs.

"I go back to Brown tomorrow," I say quietly, my voice and heart shutting down in real time.

"I know," he says sadly. He doesn't ask me how I feel. Maybe he realizes how confused I am and that hurts him like hell. Yes, looking at him now, I can see he's hurting. And I know it's because he really loves me.

I lie down beside him and nuzzle his armpit hairs with my nose. He wraps his arm around me and we fall asleep with ease, the exhaustion and anxiety over our pending goodbye a catalyst to slumber.

I wake up at four in the morning, grateful that my insomnia has bought me some more conscious time in my lover's arms. I try to breathe in every moment and etch it into my sense memory of what this feels like, this feeling of right.

At the crack of dawn, I hear my dad pull up in the Crown Vic. Of course, there's no need to leave at the crack of dawn, but that's how my dad functions. Idan is barely awake, his mind too fuzzy to process what's happening, which in a way makes things easier. I give him a long kiss on the lips, we hug, and I manage not to cry. That will happen later this afternoon.

"I love you," he says.

"I love you, too." I say, knowing now what the words truly mean.

℃℃

We ride in pseudo-silence the whole way, my dad whistling along to his classical music station, making sure to name the composer within the first few notes of every piece. He looks at me proudly when he gets them right, and for the first time I realize how much my dad hungers to be loved. I always knew his fuck-ups didn't mean he didn't love me, but it never dawned on me that he wasn't loved enough by *his* parents. He's a grown man looking for approval. From me. The roles have reversed. Hell, maybe they were always reversed.

We reach my new dorm, which is a first class upgrade from the Attica-like conditions I endured last year. This is an actual apartment in a building that feels like a real building with real tenants. Three girls will be living with me, lovely Carla being one of them.

As CPT would have it, Carla isn't here yet. The other two girls aren't either, but they have no excuse. I run through all the rooms, picking the corner one with the double windows. My dad is bringing up boxes from the car, wanting to finish this mission in record time.

I catch him smoking a cigarette, hyperventilating.

"Aba, are you okay?"

"I'm fine," he says, clutching his chest.

"I'll get the rest of the boxes. You stay here."

"Okay," he says, lighting another.

I grab it out of his hand. "Aba, you need to get your heart checked out."

"I'm fine. I swim an hour a day. I'm just exhausted. You have a lot of stuff."

"When you get back to the city, you're going to see a cardiologist."

"Iris, I'm . . . fine."

"If you don't go, Aba, don't bother calling me anymore. I won't talk to you until you get your heart checked out."

He knows my ultimatums are serious. "Fine, fine. I'll go next week."

"You're going tomorrow," I say with finality, heading upstairs to my new apartment, to wait for the girls.

40

A NEW DAWN

By the time they arrive, I've unpacked and hung a disturbing number of tapestries and knick-knacks from my trip. To my relief, the new girls are lovely. One is a redhead named Amy, who has acquired her clone in male form as a boyfriend (Testament to narcissism? Comfort with the familiar?) and the other is a six-foot-tall beautiful Nigerian woman who has almost no torso but a fantastic butt that protrudes like a shelf.

The phone rings as we finish dinner. Amy answers it.

"Iris! Dawn is on the phone for you."

"Who?"

"Dawn . . . Oh, sorry, Ee-dawn."

"Idan?"

"Yes, that sounds right."

I run to the phone. "Hey!"

"Hey!"

A pause ensues. Uh-oh. I really hope this conversation

doesn't turn weird. It's our first time talking on the phone. Weirdity is inevitable.

Luckily Idan quickly gets the conversation moving, asking endless questions about my new dorm, which I answer with fervor. After all the information is disseminated, however, another awkward pause ensues.

Emotional shmutz time. We begin the whole "I miss you, I love you" ritual. We do not, however, launch into high-pitched poopoo shmoopy poopy voices because that would be a crime worse than murder. Idan says he will wait for me as long as it takes, that I am the love of his life. I tell him he is the love of my life. I don't disclose that he is the *first* love of my life for fear that it will sound less profound. I mean, Idan's been in numerous relationships; that I am the love of his life is a big deal. Me? I've only slept around, dumping and emoting, usually in that order.

Idan kisses me over the phone. We tell each other we love each other again. I wish him a safe flight, and we hang up in perfect unison—because that's how connected we are.

The phone rings a second later. I smile. Nothing like a man wanting just one more goodbye.

"Yes, Idan?"

"Iris?"

It's my dad's wife, Meryl, and it's 11:00 p.m. My heart stops.

"What's wrong?"

"Your father's in the hospital."

"What?"

"He went to the cardiologist this afternoon. After a stress test, they rushed him into surgery for a quintuple bypass. The surgeon said that if you hadn't sent him to get tested he would have had a heart attack for certain."

My stomach pulls a Greg Louganis, slamming directly into the diving board before plummeting into the icy water.

I come up for air and tell Meryl I'll get there as soon as humanly possible, which means the first train the next morning.

I dial Idan, my fingers shaking.

Snake answers. "HEY, IRIS! WHAT'S UP?" he yells. I can almost feel the coke powder sifting through the receiver.

"Is Idan there?"

"YEAH! HOLD ON!"

I give Idan the news. He tries to be positive, but not in a fake "Everything is going to be fine, don't worry" way, which is fortunate since I'm not a fan of the "Don't worry!" school of soothing.

"At least we get to see each other again," he says sweetly.

I don't know how to respond to that. I hang up before he does.

❧

By the time I get to the hospital, my dad is post-surgery and in good spirits. He vows never to smoke again and to eat less chicken liver and egg yolks. I leave him and Meryl and rush to see Idan at the Snakehouse. I can't help being distant. It's almost as if the Idan chapter in my life has abruptly closed for me but has only begun for him. He talks about how much he missed me, how he will wait for me in Tel Aviv, how he wants to be with me. Problem is, Pop's health scare has jolted my inner-child from her blissful nap. She's never taken a nap that long before and is now freaked out that she overslept and, in her lack of vigilance, caused the bad things that are now happening. The thought of anything more serious happening between Idan and me is too much for me to handle at the moment. I can't bring myself to tell him that, so I stay withdrawn and attribute my lack of affection to the events of the last twenty-four hours. He doesn't buy it but is sensitive and caring enough to give me my space, regardless of the suffering it's causing him.

I have a long way to go. Sure, Idan has broken through some barriers, but I haven't yet reached a place where I can look at a man and not be scared of what's to come. I know now that if given another chance when the timing is right, I will be. But this isn't that time.

Idan wants me to stay the night, but I tell him I have to get back to Providence. We kiss goodbye. We both know it's real this time. He cries. I do not. I have no tears left in me.

☙

By the time I get back to the dorm, it's 2:00 a.m. I open the door quietly, and am surprised to find all three girls waiting up for me. Carla envelops me in one of her warm Jamaican hugs. The girls are truly relieved my father is okay, and I am truly relieved they are part of my life.

Carla asks me what time I have to be up tomorrow for our first day of classes.

That's right. Classes start tomorrow. Classes. Learning. The reason I came here in the first place. And you know what? I chose better this year. Neuroscience (challenging), Scandinavian Film (depressing), Abnormal Psychology (autobiographical), and Intro to Acting, where I hope to utilize my many challenging, depressing, autobiographical issues for a worthy cause: entertaining the masses.

The girls and I head to our respective bedrooms. My bed feels gloriously warm—a combo of my fuzzy flannel sheets and the heat vent. I curl into a fetal ball, images from the last three months swirling through my head: Idan's lips, falling coconuts, Iordana's tears, Talia's boobs, bloody underwear, stormy hammocks, Loco and me galloping on the ridge. The images somehow look brighter and more festive from the comfort of my current cocoon, stripped of their negatives. They linger in my mind just long enough for me to fall asleep with a smile on my face.